THE UNIVERSITY
of
UTOPIA

There are periods of decline when the pattern fades to which our inmost life must conform. When we enter upon them we sway and lose our balance. From hollow joy we sink to leaden sorrow, and past and future acquire a new charm from our sense of loss. So we wander aimlessly in the irretrievable past or in distant Utopias; but the fleeting moment we cannot grasp.

ERNST JUENGER, *On the Marble Cliffs*, trans. STUART HOOD (copyright 1947 by New Directions)

THE UNIVERSITY

of

UTOPIA

By

Robert M. Hutchins

THE UNIVERSITY OF CHICAGO PRESS

CHICAGO AND LONDON

CHARLES R. WALGREEN FOUNDATION LECTURES

THE UNIVERSITY OF CHICAGO PRESS, CHICAGO 60637
The University of Chicago Press, Ltd., London

International Standard Book Number: 0-226-3617   5

86 85 84 83 82 81 80 79   9 8 7 6 5

INTRODUCTION TO THE
SECOND EDITION

IF WE survive, we are going to live in a wantless, work-less world. The machines will do the work.

The shift from scarcity to abundance, from "full employment" to full unemployment, was predicted by Lord Keynes in 1930. He then thought the process would take one hundred years. I believe he would now cut the time in half. The rate of technological change has surpassed anything he could have foreseen.

One figure will stand for many: this year the automobile industry produced 210,000 more cars than in 1955 with 162,000 fewer workers.

If we could bring ourselves to stop wasting fifty billion dollars a year on what is laughingly called defense, we would confront the Keynesian utopia almost immediately. Even today, all our basic industries, including agriculture, are afflicted with "excess capacity."

We can do a few things, each of which involves its own brand of revolution, to postpone the day to which Lord Keynes looked forward.

We can try to see to it that all Americans are equipped with the material means of life. One-third of our population now lives at the poverty line.

We can embark on an enormous development of the public sector, building and staffing hospitals, libraries, museums, theaters, schools, colleges, universities, and research institutes. Today all our population is culturally underprivileged. Even the rich New Yorker has fewer cultural advantages and opportunities than the ordinary citizen of many European communities of modest size. Only the rich in the United States have access to the kind of medical care that comes as a matter of right to citizens of many other countries. Teachers' salaries ought to be doubled, not because all our present teachers deserve it, but because only in this way can we hope to attract the kind of teachers we need.

We can accept responsibility for the development of the developing countries. Their needs are infinite. The difficulty lies in the rate at which they can absorb assistance. In order to do this in a sensible fashion, they have to have their own ideas and leaders. These can appear only with time. Meanwhile, the productivity of the industrialized world will increase at an even faster rate.

The excess capacity of the United States is estimated at somewhere between thirty and sixty billion dollars a year. It doesn't make much difference which figure you choose. It will be larger next year. Ten billion dollars a year is probably the largest sum that can providently be expended at present in aid to the developing countries.

No matter what we do about improving the condition of our own people, about expanding the public sector, and about aid to the developing countries, we are still going to be right up against Lord Keynes's future. And of course the political difficulties of doing what we ought to do on these three fronts are such that we shall probably take no more than half-measures on any one of them.

From one point of view the Keynesian future is utopia. To repeal the primordial curse is almost by definition to return to Paradise. But this utopia, which is almost within our grasp, requires changes of the most profound order—in our outlook on life, in our slogans, in our most cherished beliefs, one of the most cherished of which is the doctrine of Salvation by Work. Second thoughts about the Keynesian utopia arouse, as Keynes said, "a certain dread."

The association of education with earning a living, and developing industrial power, which was a legitimate subject of debate when this book was written, is, a decade later, patently absurd. Everybody is now aware that the official rate of unemployment among young people is double that among adults. The actual rate is undoubtedly higher, because many young people have thought it useless to apply for work. The general reaction to this situation borders on fantasy: it is to propose widespread extension of vocational training. In short, the cure for the disease of no jobs is training for them.

One who has faith that man is in some degree rational, though in great degree animal, must believe that sooner or later the light will shine through the murk. Sometime we shall understand that what we are after is wisdom, and we shall try to reform our educational system in order to get it. We might begin by thinking seriously, now, about the establishment of the University of Utopia.

Santa Barbara, California

ix

FOREWORD

Mr. hutchins' outstanding contributions to American education in theory and practice are producing profound changes in higher education. In most of our colleges and universities some plan of general education prior to specialized training has already been, or is in the process of being, established. It would not be an exaggeration to say that this movement owes as much to Mr. Hutchins as to any person in American life today.

The present work represents lectures given by Mr. Hutchins under the auspices of the Charles R. Walgreen Foundation for the Study of American Institutions at the University of Chicago in the spring of 1953. It draws a picture of the operation of the best of universities in the best of countries. Its purpose is to provide a standard by which to measure our aims and accomplishments. This is not a flight into the ethereal realms of fancy but a practical guide for courageous educators who know that to cure our educational ills requires radical surgery, not homeopathic remedies.

Jerome G. Kerwin
Chairman, Walgreen Foundation

CONTENTS

I

INDUSTRIALIZATION

THIS book is about the hazards to education in the United States. Education in the United States is a wonderful thing. But it faces at the moment certain peculiar dangers. The principal ones seem to be those associated with industrialization, specialization, philosophical diversity, and social and political conformity. Industrialization seems to charm people into thinking that the prime aim of life and hence of education is the development of industrial power. Specialization has dire effects upon the effort to build up a community and particularly a community of the learned. Philosophical diversity raises the question whether a community is possible. Social and political conformity, on the other hand, suggests that the kind of community we seem to be headed for is one that we shall not like when we get it.

I shall hope to indicate methods by which these hazards can be overcome. In doing so, I shall have occasion from time to time to refer to the accomplishments of Utopia, a country that has faced the same dangers and that has, it seems to me, produced an intelligible educational system in spite of them. Perhaps I should tell you now a little about Utopia. Utopia is not Heaven. It is inhabited by people much like ourselves. It is a country in the Western world. Its climate resembles that of southern California, though

there is no other resemblance. It is a scientific, industrial democracy. It is rich and powerful. It is surrounded by enemy states. It is committed to the doctrine of education for all. Its principal educational
problem has been to determine how to educate everybody so that the country may have the scientific and
industrial strength it requires and at the same time
educate everybody so that the country will know
how to use its scientific and industrial power wisely.
I hope that the masterly solution of this problem at
which the Utopians have arrived may commend itself
to you. At the end I shall inquire whether it is possible
for the United States, which has the same problem,
to adopt the same solution.

Industrialization obviously affects the conditions
under which education is given. It provides relative
wealth and relative leisure. It makes large expenditures
on education possible. In its early stages it has drastic
effects on the content of education as well as on the
conditions in which education operates. When industrial development begins in an underdeveloped
country, the pressure toward technical training is
naturally very great. The effort is to get everybody
into the state of mind that will make him fit readily
into the developing industrial framework. Before universal, free, compulsory education this effort was of
course not conducted through the educational system.
The mass of the workers was drawn from a class that
had never had educational opportunities. The economic necessities of that class required them to allow
their children to enter industry, or even to force them
into it, at a tender age. The combination of the desire

of industrialists for a supply of cheap labor and the necessities of the working class led to those horrors in the evolution of capitalism accurately described by Karl Marx.

In England and America the evolution of the industrial system was accompanied by universal suffrage and universal education. These countries did not construct their educational systems in order to have a place to put the children they wanted to take out of industry. They inaugurated universal education in order to prepare the rising generation for universal suffrage. Lord Sherbrooke expressed the view common in aristocratic circles in England after the passage of the second Reform Bill when he said, "Now we must educate our masters." In this country the expressions of the Founding Fathers about universal education leave no doubt that their motive was the same: they believed that a democratic country could not survive unless the people were educated to use the suffrage wisely. I think this is the prevailing attitude in England today. The object of the educational system, taken as a whole, is not to produce hands for industry or to teach the young how to make a living.[1] It is to produce responsible citizens.

1. "I think that it is very important for the future of Africa that we should hold fast to the idea that the function of education is to take boys and girls and develop them as human beings to the highest possibility that they have: to train them to make the best use of their gifts. There are still some people who say that agriculture is so important for Africa—and I agree that it is vitally important—that the educational system should aim at producing good village folk. I cannot agree. It is not the job of education to teach people to know their proper stations and to stay in them. We have rejected that idea of education in this country, and it

When you want to have universal, free, compulsory education, and you want to have it all at once, the educational difficulties that you confront are very serious. Think of the task of merely housing an educational system for everybody in a large country. Where can you find competent teachers in sufficient numbers? And what will the system do with all the new young people, many of them without background or interest, whom the legislature has suddenly thrown upon it? If the country is one that is committed to building up its industrial power, and if it is one in which success is identified with success in earning a living, then the needs of the individual and the needs of society will seem to coincide in demanding that the young be prepared to work in industry.

The paradox is that, the more industrialized a country becomes, the less it needs technical training of the kind usually supplied at the lower levels of education. I think it easy to demonstrate that technical training does not and cannot meet the needs of the individual or of society, even assuming that those needs are what they are supposed to be. Technical training cannot help an individual to be a success, and it cannot help industry to prosper. When industrialization and mechanization have reached a high point, they minimize the necessity for such training. The object of mechanization is not merely to save labor; it is also to reduce, through continuous simplifica-

has no place in Africa. If we are short of miners in Britain we do not look to the schools to train them: we look to the Coal Board to attract them by better pay and housing, baths and canteens. And we shall have to attract Africans to the land in similar ways" (W. E. F. Ward, *The Listener*, July 9, 1953, p. 54).

tion, the amount of training that is necessary to operate machines. The rapidity with which industrial corporations trained men in the last war shows what can be done when technology has arrived at the stage that it has attained in the United States.

If industrialists today indicate that they want workers trained in the schools, as some of them constantly say they do, it is because they are misguided. In Pasadena there is a fight going on between the operators of foundries and the Pasadena City College. The foundry operators say that they need trained workers and that it is the duty of the College to supply them. The College has a course for foundry workers but wishes to abandon it because it loses money—it has too few students. The foundry operators reply that there would be plenty of students if the College properly advertised the course, as it is the duty of the College to do. It is interesting to note that in this controversy nobody has raised the question why it is the responsibility of a tax-supported college to train the foundry operators' hands for them or what the educational content of a course for foundry workers is. It is simply assumed that a college should meet the needs that any part of the industrial system has for workers and meet the needs that any individual feels to be trained in anything. The only question is, therefore, whether there is a need. If a need is identified, the educational system must meet it. If this involves the actual recruiting of a labor force for an industry, the educational system must recruit it.

I have not been able to reconcile these conclusions with the theory of free enterprise, under which, one would think, the business of making an occupation attractive and training neophytes to practice it should devolve upon the enterpriser and not upon institutions supported by taxpayers or philanthropists. We simply assume that industrial development is so important and the need for economic training so fundamental that the public interest in paying the public's money for the support of these objects may be taken for granted.

The fact is, of course, that the Pasadena foundry operators, if they undertook to train their workers themselves, would be better satisfied in the end. The standard method of preparing workers for industry, before the advent of universal and prolonged education, was to put them to work. The difficulty in creating in any kind of school an adequate imitation of an industrial situation and the rapid and accelerating technical development of our time present the problem that confronts anybody who thinks he can do an effective job of preparing workers in any other way than by putting them to work.

But there is something more serious here than the mere inefficiency of technical training. Industrialization and mechanization alter the conditions of life, and hence, of education, through the dehumanization of work. When the assembly line becomes the characteristic instrument of production, when a man stands eight hours a day automatically repeating the same operation, which may be no more than pushing the same button over and over again, when he becomes in effect merely a part of a machine, the conditions of his life represent a dramatic departure from those which the craftsman or farmer knew in earlier days.

The educational system must, if possible, take these changes into account. It must, if possible, find ways of enriching life on the assembly line and ways of enriching the time that a man does not spend on the assembly line. The problem of making work significant in an industrial, mechanized economy is one of the most difficult in the modern world. It will not do to say, as I have said many times, that this problem can be solved by the steady reduction in the hours of labor and by giving significance to free time. Free time should have significance, and to this issue I shall turn in a moment. But as long as people have to spend any considerable fraction of their lives in work, what they work at, and how they work at it, ought to have as much meaning for them and do as much for them as possible.

It seems unlikely that any form of vocational or technical training can help give significance to life on the assembly line. Such significance could be achieved only by understanding the processes through which the worker was going, through understanding the relation of those processes to the processes in which other workers were engaged, through understanding the contribution made by the efforts of the worker to the product, and through understanding the significance of the product in the economic and social situation. The man on the assembly line, if he is to be a man, must have something in his head. No society that made any claim to be enlightened could contemplate the possibility that any section of its population could be reduced to subhuman status.

The steady reduction in the hours of labor has undoubtedly offered new opportunities to the man on the assembly line. He now has about twenty hours a week more free time than his grandfather had. This time could be used to increase his understanding of the significance of his work and to promote his development as a human being. Liberals since the dawn of the industrial era have insisted on the reduction of the hours of labor because they had these ends in view. I sometimes think that the bitterness that liberals feel toward radio, television, and the other so-called media of mass communication results from their disappointment at what the man on the assembly line has done with the free time that they have helped him to obtain.

Although we should not underestimate the growing interest in art and music in this country, in general the free time the worker has gained has meant more time to waste. New methods of wasting it and new objects to waste it upon are being invented every day. The worker who previously had only a little time in which to get drunk, beat his wife, or go to burlesque shows now has much more time to get drunk, beat his wife, and watch television. No wonder the liberals feel betrayed.

They feel betrayed likewise by the results of universal, free, compulsory education, which, like the reduction in the hours of labor, has been a foundation stone of liberalism since the earliest times. Universal education, instead of fulfilling the hopes of its sponsors by liberating the worker and enabling him to get political power and use it wisely, has made him the victim of charlatans in every field of human activity. The people have received, as a result of the movement toward universal education, just enough education to permit them to be victimized by advertising and propaganda, not enough to enable them to appraise and resist the arts of those who have been engaged in depriving them of the political power their education was to give them.

The nature of the education that the people have received has contributed also to the continuous enlargement of the area of wasted time. There has been little in their education to suggest that time should not be wasted or to propose methods of employing it usefully. Only an education conceived of as moral, intellectual, aesthetic, and spiritual growth could accomplish these aims. An education dedicated, for example, to training a boy to earn a living cannot lay the basis for the useful employment of those hours of his life in which he is not earning a living.

In the United States the habits formed in childhood and youth are likely to have a determining influence upon the employment of free time in adult life; for there are no compelling motives in the life of American adults to draw them irresistibly into the kind of activities that should characterize the free, independent, developing human being. There is tremendous pressure toward conformity in the United States. There is tremendous pressure toward success, which is usually interpreted to mean money, power, and publicity. There is little effective pressure toward moral, intellectual, aesthetic, and spiritual growth.

The motives that have induced large numbers of adults in other countries to go on learning after they have left school do not exist in the United States. Those motives have been to obtain political power, to gain social advancement, or to make more money. In the United States education is irrelevant to all these objects, with the exception that certain formal educational requirements must be met in order to gain entrance to certain occupations. These requirements are not normally such as to lay any basis for interest in continued learning in adult life.

As universal, free, compulsory education spread gradually over western Europe, as new standards of formal education were established for the children of the citizens, many adults, who had reached maturity at an earlier stage of educational history, found themselves without the education that their children were expected to have and unable to meet the new standards. As more and more formal education came to be expected as a requirement for entrance into certain occupations, it was naturally regarded as unjust that those who through the accident of birth or fortune had not had an opportunity to obtain the necessary qualifications should be debarred from the opportunity to gain a livelihood for this reason. The gradual enfranchisement of the population of Europe and the United Kingdom in the last century led the leaders of society to forward the education of adults as a safeguard to their institutions and led the workers to interest themselves in it as a means of laying hands on political power. Since education had been limited to those who had prestige as well as power, it was assumed that the avenue to prestige, as well as power, was education. In some countries the movement toward adult education was assisted by the desire to remedy certain special evils, in Sweden the evil of drink, and in Denmark the sense of national degradation that resulted from the defeat by Germany in 1864.

In the United States today there is no sense of special emergency that could be met through the continued learning of adults. Social advancement is not dependent upon education. Political power of the ordinary democratic kind comes to the individual as he reaches the age of twenty-one. In achieving political power beyond that, education is probably a handicap rather than an advantage. I cannot imagine a candidate for office in the United States suggesting that he is entitled to the suffrages of his fellow-citizens because he is better educated than his opponent. On the other hand, I have no difficulty in imagining a candidate asking for votes on the ground that he is rougher and tougher than his opponent and that he does not have any big thoughts or know any long words. While high employment at high wages persists, the educational requirements for entrance into various occupations, though they are annoying, and for the most part irrational, do not constitute a major obstacle to the prosperity and happiness of the bulk of the population.

There is no doubt that education must be useful. It

must meet the needs of the individual and of society. The question is: What are those needs? Or, more particularly, what are the real needs of the individual and of society and which of them can education meet? In many ages it has been thought that education could make its greatest contribution by helping people learn to think and by familiarizing them with the intellectual tradition in which they live. This assumption was current in the Western world one hundred and fifty years ago and still held the field a century ago. It was perhaps the dominant view in the United States up to 1900.

Some of the most magniloquent passages in Cardinal Newman's *Idea of a University* are those in which he celebrates the true usefulness of liberal education. But the fact that he felt constrained to enter upon such flights of oratory in the middle of the last century shows how strong even in his day was the tendency to hold that usefulness could mean only usefulness to the rising industrial and financial power of Britain. No one stopped long to inquire whether educational institutions could give instruction that would actually be useful in this sense or whether the society of Britain, which was rapidly becoming industrial, scientific, and technological, needed thinking about important subjects and acquaintance with its tradition any the less because of these developments. The doctrine of Adam Smith began to tell: it was the duty of every man to make as much money as he could; in the process he would be led as by an Invisible Hand to promote the common good. It was assumed that the needs of the community would best be advanced by the rapid expansion of industry and technology. Thomas Mann's novel, *Buddenbrooks*, shows the same process going on in Germany at about the same time.

Meanwhile liberal education was associated in the public mind with a pre-industrial, pre-scientific, pre-democratic era. It was an anachronism, and an aristocratic anachronism at that. It was possible to attack it as frivolous, irrelevant, and decorative. It was like a medieval ruin occupying valuable space in a busy market place. Besides, it did not seem to pay.

We are now familiar with the notion that the real strength of a nation lies in its industrial power. The German and Japanese adventures were built on this premise. Although the failure of these experiments is not conclusive evidence of the falsity of the premise, for perhaps Germany and Japan simply misjudged their power, their failure may suggest to us, as indeed all history suggests, that something more than power is needed if a nation is to become and continue to be successful in any meaning of the word. The indispensable ingredient is wisdom.

It is impossible to suppose that an educational system dedicated to industrial power can produce the wisdom that a country needs to use its power in its own best interests, to say nothing of those of the human race. There does not appear to be any necessary connection between industrial power and wisdom, nor does it seem to be absolutely essential that a man be wise in order to become an industrial leader. Like a natural force, industrial power is neutral. It may be used for good or evil, for self-preservation or suicide. The delusions of grandeur that it seems almost inevitably to carry with it tend rather to suicide than self-preservation.

Whatever may have been the case in earlier times or in other types of society, the wisdom that a democratic community needs is the wisdom of the entire population. When the few rule the state, it may be sufficient if they are wise. When the whole people are the ultimate rulers, nothing less than a wise people will do. Then the man on the assembly line, the farmer, the lawyer, the doctor, the engineer, or the housewife has to have ready a contribution to the common store of wisdom. A democracy must have leaders—but its leaders are selected by the people and governed by them.

This may suggest to us certain reflections on the nature of strength in a democratic society. In such a society true strength lies in the character of the citizens. This means the moral, intellectual, aesthetic, and spiritual level they have reached, their grasp of and devotion to the hierarchy of values for which their country stands. In this view one of the most important elements in the strength of a country, if not the most important, is its educational system. But this view rests on the assumption that the educational system will be directed to moral, intellectual, aesthetic, and spiritual growth and by a hierarchy of values. With these things an educational system aiming at industrial power does not seem likely to be concerned.

If industrial power is the object, the best education is scientific, not vocational or technical. The object of a scientific education is to understand the natural world, not to manipulate it. Scientific education is not open to the objection that it cannot accomplish what it pretends to do, an objection that is fatal to vocational and technical training. Through a scientific education a student can come to understand the natural world; through vocational or technical training he is likely to be unfitted for the operations for which he has been trained. He may be confronted with entirely new machines or an entirely new industrial situation; he may, in a country where the population is highly fluid, have to earn his living in a way or in a place of which he and his teachers never dreamed. In a fluid, industrial, scientific democracy, the more specific an education is, the less likely it is to achieve the only purpose that it has—to prepare the student for a particular kind of economic activity. In a fluid, industrial, scientific democracy, if education is general or liberal, it will at least not interfere with the economic progress of the man who has it. In such a society the study of science will lead to success in the sense in which the term is commonly used, and it will promote the industrial power of the society.

Science is perhaps the greatest accomplishment of modern times. Against its notable and undoubted contributions to the progress of mankind must be counted certain side effects, for which, in general, neither science nor scientists are responsible, but which have had serious consequences for modern thought and education. The reverence that science has inspired has led scholars in other disciplines, seeking equally notable results and equally high prestige, to apply the method of science to subject matters to which it is not appropriate. Only trivial results can be accomplished by these means. Science has trivialized other fields of learning.

What we are looking for is wisdom, and it does not seem sensible to say that the insights and understanding offered us by the greatest creations of the human mind cannot help us in our search. Homer was the teacher of Greece. It would be a bold man who would say that Newton had taught the West more than Shakespeare.

We can say the same of the great historians, philosophers, and theologians. They have labored by methods of their own to tell us what they have observed about man, society, the world, and God. We need to know, for example, whether God exists. It makes a difference. Will it be seriously argued that science can ever give us the answer to this question or that, if it cannot, the question is unimportant?

The natural sciences deal with the material conditions of existence and have had profound effects upon those conditions. The relationship of science and industrial power is enough to make the point. The accomplishments of natural science have been such as to convince us that infinite improvement in the material conditions of existence is possible if only we will concentrate our attention on this improvement. All we have to do to grasp this phenomenon is to contrast the position of the artist today with that which he occupied in the Renaissance. The technology that is based upon science lends itself to the production of vast quantities of material goods. Since industrialization got under way in the West, the doctrine has been that the intelligence and energy of mankind should be devoted to increasing the quantity of such goods. Now the West is preaching the same doctrine to the East, and the East seems altogether too likely to embrace it. As I have said, this is not the fault of science or of scientists. It would, however, have been impossible without them. In the process quality has been sacrificed to quantity, and the arts have become a mere decoration, or a recreation for females not gainfully employed.

I lately heard a leading American industrialist comment upon proposals to send American art and letters abroad so that Europeans could get some idea of the cultural life of this country. If I understood him correctly, he said that Europeans had the arts and literature and that they were proud of them and should be encouraged to go on with them and to send them over here. We, on the other hand, had an entirely materialistic or mechanistic civilization. We should be proud of it and should go on with it. We should send our machines and the vast array of consumer goods that they produce to Europe and receive back culture in exchange.

This theory of continental specialization shows how far we have come from any defensible view of the aims of life and of organized society. Art and thought are the highest activities of man. They are the aims of life, and society should be organized to promote them first of all. It is a sign of a backward civilization when in a financial crisis the first thing

the community thinks of is to close the art museums
and reduce expenditures on education. A civilization
without art and thought, or one that does not value
them, is a pack rather than a civilization. The remarks
of the industrialist I have quoted reflect an unthink-
able and intolerable view of American society, for
what rational person would care to inhabit a country
where all that made life worth living had to be im-
ported?

The distinguishing characteristic of the people of
Utopia is their common sense. Common sense is no
longer very common elsewhere. In nothing do they
exhibit this characteristic more clearly than in their
capacity and determination to call things by their
right names and put them in their proper places. This
capacity and determination seem to result from the
Utopians' habit of asking themselves at all times what
they are trying to do. As a consequence of this process of self-interrogation the Utopians have concluded
that industrial power, military strength, longer life,
and an infinity of gadgets cannot constitute, singly or
together, the aims of human life or of organized society. The Utopians recognize the importance of industrial strength and military power. They are grateful to the scientists for providing them with a longer
life. They are of two minds about gadgets. On the
one hand, they notice with interest that these devices
have in many cases increased the leisure available to
the people. On the other, they observe with some
alarm that the charm of these devices promotes infan-
tilism in the population, that their multiplication may
consume a disproportionate share of the resources and

energies of the country, and that some of them, because of the horrible sounds or pictures they are capable of emitting, or because they are dangerous when in motion in large numbers, may be destructive of the leisure that they could create and even of life itself.

The Utopians cannot conceive that the aims of their lives are to produce industrial strength, military power, or more gadgets. They do not even believe that they are here to exert a favorable influence upon the mortality tables. They do not see that industrial strength, military power, longer life, or more gadgets would be beneficial if they did not know what to do with them. They think that their educational system ought to have some role in helping them to determine what to do with these things when they get them. They do not believe that an educational system aiming at industrial strength, military power, longer life, or more gadgets will, by any stretch of the imagination, help the people learn what to do with them.

The Utopians encourage science because they want to understand the world, live longer, and have industrial strength. They do not encourage industry, because they take free enterprise seriously. Nor do they encourage industrialists, no matter how powerful or how wealthy, to believe that they are, because of their industrial achievements, the natural leaders of the community, qualified to determine its policies, manage its institutions, and express its ideals. The highest honors conferred by the state go not to those who have got rich through the production and sale of gadgets but to those whom Utopia delights to honor, its artists and thinkers.

The reason why the Utopians reserve their highest honors for their most distinguished thinkers and artists is that they believe that thought and art are the highest activities of the human race. They do not see that the purpose of society is to help men make a profit through the production and sale of anything. The Utopians are not fools. They know that economic and industrial strength and military power go together. They know that all are necessary to a healthy society, at least in a world like the one we live in. They believe that the incentives supplied through the free-enterprise system are adequate to induce sufficient interest in the development of economic and industrial strength. The incentives to art and thought, which are activities of the most painful and difficult kind, cannot and should not be exclusively financial, though the Utopians think it wise to spend on these objects at least as much as the national budget for liquor, cosmetics, and chewing gum. The encouragement to art and thought on which the Utopians principally rely is the honor universally accorded them.

Thus in Utopia industrial strength and military power, efforts to lengthen life and to distribute gadgets, scientific training and liberal education—all fall into place. The Utopians have never been misled into thinking that technical training from the elementary school onward can create industrial power. They do not believe that science is the only knowledge worth having. They are not confused about what makes a country strong. They rely on their patriotism, moral fervor, and intellectual capacity, which, they hold, gives them the ability to meet any new situation with intelligence and decision. Their hope is to be wise and to become so through their educational system.

II

SPECIALIZATION

SCIENCE splits things up into smaller and smaller pieces. Specialization is the life of science. The more specialized a scientific institution is, the better it is likely to be.

A scientific department in a university is a large collection of specialists living in a tent twenty-five to fifty years old the name of which has little or no connection with what goes on inside it. Think of the name "physiology," "chemistry," or "anatomy" as we used to understand it a generation ago and compare the connotations of it then with the activities that physiologists, chemists, and anatomists carry on today. The names of these departments are hereditary titles that have no more significance than such appellations now carry with them in political life. But, though they have little significance in describing the work that is done under their auspices, they have considerable importance in the lives of those who progress through these departments and receive their degrees.

A university department, in general, seems to justify its existence as a kind of guild or trade-union. The department's name need have little connection with the work that is done in the department. Some departments of literature seem to be departments of history, linguistics, or philosophy. But the candidates for higher degrees in these departments have to get jobs in other departments in the same field and must receive insignia generally recognizable in the academic world. We know that there are departments of English and that they will employ Ph.D.'s in English. They will employ nobody else. If a candidate for the Ph.D. in English gets interested in Jonathan Edwards and studies history, philosophy, and theology and knows nothing whatever about English literature, he must still get his Ph.D. in English and still get a job in an English department somewhere. There are no departments of Jonathan Edwards and none in which history, philosophy, and theology form a respectable combination.

Such names as physiology, chemistry, and anatomy, to which may be added the names of many other scientific departments, imply an understanding of some considerable field of knowledge. The activities of departments bearing these names carry no such implications. It is not necessary for a professor in these fields, to say nothing of a graduate student, to understand the subject as a whole, and it may be a positive disadvantage to him to try to do so. The scientist succeeds through splitting off a manageable fragment of the natural world and submitting it to thorough examination. The fragments get smaller and smaller; specialization becomes narrower and narrower. The better a scientific department is in terms of the scientific eminence of its members, the more "productive" it is in terms of the volume of research turned out, the larger and more expensive it is, the more likely it is to be composed of extremely specialized persons training persons still more specialized.

As I have said, this is fine for the advancement of science, if by that phrase we mean the acquisition of more and more detailed knowledge about the world. But the success of this process in natural science has not been without its disadvantages to education. I take it that the aim of education is not to gain more and more detailed knowledge of the world but to understand the world and ourselves in it. If we split the world up in order to gain detailed knowledge of it, at some point we have to put it together again in order to understand it. This is not likely to be done by modern experimental scientists or any aggregation of them.

One reason it cannot be done by any aggregation of them is that they cannot understand one another. This is a deprivation to them as scientists, or at least it would seem so; for it would appear that a man ought to be a better scientist if he could understand science and other scientists. But the extreme specialization that is natural, inevitable, and to some extent desirable in experimental science has aroused the enthusiastic imitation of scholars in other fields, where it is unnatural, avoidable, and wholly undesirable.

The reverence that natural science has inspired is in large part responsible for the steady narrowing of education that the progress of specialization has caused during the last thirty years. The progress of specialization has meant that the world and ourselves have been progressively taken apart, and at no point have they been put together again. As the progress of the scientific method has discredited the methods of history, philosophy, and art, so the specialism essential to science has discredited a generalized approach to history, philosophy, art, and all other subjects, including science itself. This means that comprehension has been discredited; for it cannot be attained by splitting the world into smaller and smaller bits.

Every important scientific discovery produces innumerable new specialties. New lines of investigation open up. Men must be trained to follow them. Since we can see no end to scientific progress, we can see no limit to the multiplication of scientific specialties and the demand for specialists trained specifically for the new specialties that appear.

In terms of the size of the total population, however, the number of specialists that science will require is very small indeed. Industrialization and mechanization, built on science and technology, inevitably tend to reduce the proportion of specialists that the society as a whole can find use for. The man on the assembly line, repeating almost automatically the same simple operation all day long, is the goal toward which mechanization tends. Thus, though the absolute number of specialists needed to keep science, technology, and industry moving forward will increase, the relative demand for specialists will decline.

I am not denying that there may be many new ways of earning a living, many new occupations growing out of new discoveries, inventions, and demands. I am asserting that the total time of training required for specialized or differentiated occupations, for ways of earning a living, must steadily shrink as mechanization advances. As mechanization advances, whole occupations may be swept out of existence.

I have no doubt that somewhere in the country there is a school or junior college that has a course for pinboys in bowling alleys and that its administration and faculty are now looking with alarm at the new machine that must inevitably drive the pinboys out of the alleys, never to return. I still anxiously await the full effect of what I believe is called the "home permanent" upon the innumerable courses in what is called "cosmetology" offered by the schools, junior colleges, and colleges of the state of California.

I saw the other day in Berkeley something I had never expected to see in my life. I saw a Doctor of Philosophy in Driver Education. No pupil in the schools of California may graduate without taking a course in how to drive an automobile. These courses have to have teachers. The teachers have to take courses in methods of teaching how to drive an automobile. The teachers of these teachers have to be professors in colleges or universities. Professors in colleges and universities have to have the Ph.D. Therefore in California there have to be Ph.D.'s in Driver Education. The one I saw was a very good driver (see p. 27).

Anyone who has ridden on the roads of California can understand why the people of that state should want to make sure that the rising generation learns how to drive, just as anyone who has seen a forest fire can understand why courses in fire prevention are

UNIVERSITY OF COLORADO EXTENSION DIVISION
AT BOULDER

Invites Your Participation in the Class

DRIVER EDUCATION IN THE SECONDARY SCHOOLS—Education 409-2

Course Description:

This is the basic course in driver education which prepares the teacher to administer a driver education and training program on the high-school level. The class is designed to acquaint the driver-training teacher with the methods and materials found effective in such a program and to help make their schools eligible to obtain a dual-control car for use in their program.

The course includes the following topics:
Driver characteristics and their implication
Familiarization and use of classroom materials
Effective methods of behind-the-wheel instruction
Use of audio-visual aids
Psychophysical devices used in testing
Written tests and program evaluation
Administrative problems and procedures in a driver education
  program
Skill exercises in driving
Educational implications of modern traffic and safety problems

Schedule:

Classes will be held from 2:40 to 4:40 P.M. Monday, Tuesday, Wednesday, Thursday, and Friday afternoons. Two evening sessions will be scheduled at the convenience of those enrolling. Classes will begin July 27 and end August 21. Classes will be held in Hellems 101.

Credit:

Two semester hours of undergraduate extension credit. Such credit will satisfy in part the methods requirement of teachers completing the B.A. or B.S. degrees and receiving a state teaching certificate. All students satisfactorily completing this class will be presented with an AAA certificate qualifying them to receive a dual-control car for use in their school program.

Tuition:

$15.00 for Colorado residents. $18.00 for nonresidents.

Instructor:

Mr. Leo Lewis, director of driver education at the University of Colorado Extension Division and instructor in adult driver training for the University Extension Division.

Registration:

For registration and further information come to Woodbury Hall, Room 103, before the first class on Monday, July 27.

required in California. Does it automatically follow
that the educational system of a community should
try to meet whatever needs the community thinks
are pressing? Is there no other way to see to it that
young people learn to drive or to refrain from throwing lighted cigarettes into the woods? If the community thinks it needs beauticians or if the young
ladies of the community think that they need to
become beauticians, is the educational system the
only or the best place in which these needs can be
gratified? These questions can be answered only if we
can get some more rational view than we have at present of the purpose of education and how education
fits in with other social institutions.

At the lower levels of education in America the
tendency toward overspecialization seems to result
from the frustration of teachers, themselves ill-prepared, confronting enormous crowds of ill-prepared
and uninterested pupils, in a society that has come to
regard earning a living as the first, if not the whole,
duty of man and that has learned from John Dewey
that the young can be interested and educated best
through the study of occupations.

John Dewey's authority cannot be cited on behalf
of specialized education, still less of vocational training, which he regarded as narrow and illiberal. Looking at an industrial society, he concluded that the
young should understand it and that they should do
so through considering the various economic activities
of life in their moral, political, social, and scientific
context. He also thought that this would be very interesting to them. His psychology appears to be false

and his program impractical. At least it has never been tried.

But through a natural misunderstanding it has been assumed that, when Mr. Dewey said that education could best be acquired through the study of occupations, he meant that the best education was that which prepared the pupil for an occupation. This notion was the balm in Gilead for which frustrated teachers and parents were seeking; it seemed to provide the necessary philosophical indorsement of what they wanted to do anyway. They wanted to train young people for occupations because they did not know what else to do with them. Think how hard it is to get a large group of reluctant and recalcitrant children to learn to read and write and figure and interest themselves in the tradition in which they live. Though children do not care very much about the life around them, and particularly about its economic aspects, their parents are obsessed with the notion that they must eventually make their way in the world and that their education ought to have something to do with this process.

It is impossible for us, the products of an industrial age, to imagine the degree of security provided by the family, the village, the guild, and the customs of Europe in earlier times and in the Middle and Far East today. The business of casting out the young to shift for themselves is a nineteenth-century novelty. The activities of labor unions and social reformers may be regarded as an attempt to recover pre-industrial security for the proletariat. In an industrial age the community must hope that the young when cast loose will be able to make themselves independent. If they do not, the community has no traditional way of taking care of them. Hence earning a living becomes the first duty of man.

This notion is reinforced by the common opinion that a man who does not succeed fails by his own fault. During the great depression, when people were thrown out of work all over the world by events over which they had not the slightest control, one could still see, in the attitude toward the relief of the unemployed, how persistent and powerful was the view that a man who was not able to support himself and his family was in some way to blame. Since parents do not want their children to grow up to be social pariahs, they must feel that everything is being done during childhood and youth to make these children economically independent.

Today the United States is the easiest country in the world in which to earn a living. When the economic machine works, there is high employment. When it falters, the state keeps the population alive. Yet because of the phenomenon summed up in the phrase of a Chicago professor, cultural lag, we still think that the first duty of the educational system is to help young people to learn to make a living. Actually the only way in which education can help a young person make a living, or a better living than he would make without education, is to help him meet the formal educational requirements for entrance into certain occupations. The number of occupations that have such requirements is steadily increasing, and the number of years that must be spent in school to meet them is steadily being raised.

The great bulk of the students in American universities are there in order to meet these requirements. The public acquiesces in them, first, because it is accustomed to acquiesce in the demands of pressure groups and, second, because it has a vague feeling that the members of certain occupations at least should be certified, or sanctified, in some way before they are let loose upon the public. The public is unwilling, often for good reasons, to trust these occupations to certify their own members. The universities acquiesce in these arrangements because they wish to increase their enrolments; students bring in income, and anyway there is a general feeling that excellence in educational institutions, as in most other things, increases in proportion to size. The trades, occupations, businesses, and professions promote these arrangements in order to restrict competition and enhance their prestige.

Since I believe that everybody can and should learn, I should welcome any method by which people are seduced into forming the habit of learning. Unfortunately, most of the programs of schools called "professional" have little to do with learning, because they have no visible intellectual content. There is nothing to learn. Many programs that nominally aim to prepare people for occupations have little to do with the kind of learning required in the occupation. Still others simply duplicate work offered elsewhere in the university, usually doing it less well than it is done in the nonprofessional departments and thus degrading, confusing, and impoverishing the university.

It is, of course, possible to learn something from anything. It is even possible to learn something from anybody. If the teacher is a genius, he can draw the most significant lessons from the most trivial occasions. Since the number of geniuses in the educational system must always remain limited, it seems unwise to frame a program of study from which learning can take place only if they illuminate its subject matter. In the hands of ordinary teachers trivialities must always be trivial. The educational program for school janitors at Teachers College, Columbia, or for majorettes at the University of Oklahoma, or for beauticians at Pasadena City College, or for circus performers at Florida State University, or for teachers of driving in the University of California might be truly educational if Socrates were the teacher; for he, beginning with incidents in the life of a janitor, majorette, beautician, clown, or chauffeur, would undoubtedly end with the deepest philosophical conclusions about the organization of society and the destiny of man. Of course, he would not be accepted as a teacher in any of these programs, because he would never have bothered to acquire the necessary "professional" qualifications. The teachers who have these qualifications and who are accepted must find the task of developing intellectual content out of such unpromising materials far beyond their power.

Many occupations deal with intellectual subjects—

subjects that can be thought about by ordinary people. Teaching is an obvious example. But teaching, like many other occupations, has no intellectual content in its own right. Education is not itself a discipline; it is a practical activity, a means by which the content of disciplines is communicated to those unfamiliar with it. Education is a secondary, dependent subject. It depends on what you want and what you can do. What you want depends on your philosophy. What you can do depends on your circumstances. Wherever you touch education, it fades into something else. The aims of an educational system are the aims of the society in which it is conducted. The philosophy of education is merely moral and political philosophy. Educational psychology is nothing but the psychology of learning. When we pass from the general subject of education to the more particular one of teaching, we are no better off. The teacher has to have knowledge but not knowledge of education or what purports to be knowledge about methods of teaching gained from texts prepared by professors of Education in universities. The teacher has to have knowledge of the subject that he is attempting to teach. In addition, it will be helpful if he knows how to read, write, speak, and figure. It will be helpful, in short, if he knows the liberal arts, which are the arts of communication.

The requirement for teaching in the elementary and secondary schools is a certain number of courses in Education. The requirement for college and university teaching is the Ph.D. degree. The courses in Education, in so far as they are specifically courses in how to teach or in the organization of the educational system, are notably lacking in content and could in no event have meaning for a person who had never taught. The Ph.D. degree may have some relation to preparation for specialized research, but it has none to college teaching or to any of the activities in which college teachers commonly engage.

These requirements seem to have little bearing upon the actual work of the teacher. Nor have they much more upon the formation of the habit of learning. I do not concede that courses in Education or the labor required for the Ph.D. is likely to form the habit of learning or even the habit of research, and I think no one would contend that either has much bearing on moral, intellectual, aesthetic, and spiritual growth.

What a teacher needs is a liberal education and special preparation in the subject or subjects that he may be called upon to teach. This preparation should not be such as to render him an uneducated man or one incapable of contributing to the education of others. I defy anybody to show that the Ph.D. degree in its usual manifestations has had any but a baleful effect on the colleges of liberal arts to which most of those who hold it go. The most striking change in the liberal arts colleges over the last fifty years is the multiplication of courses, the multiplication of departments, and the reduction in the intellectual scope of the individual teacher. In a liberal arts college fifty years ago the professor of history could take the work of the professor of literature if the professor of literature got sick. Now, if the professor of American history gets sick, the professor of English history cannot take his work. And in a university, if the professor of American history from 1860 to 1864 gets sick, the professor of American history from 1865 to 1870 cannot take his work.

I am not recommending that professors be regarded as interchangeable parts; I am not suggesting that specialized training is useless or unnecessary in specialized fields. You certainly want a man who has special preparation in his subject. You would also like to feel that he was a person who had had and could communicate the kind of education for which a college of liberal arts is supposed to stand. If he has had such an education plus special preparation in his field and if, before he is let loose upon the public, he has had practice in teaching under supervision, he would have a better chance of doing what the liberal arts teacher ought to do than the uneducated holder of the Ph.D.

What the prospective research worker needs is a liberal education, special preparation in the subject in which he plans to carry on research, and practice in research under supervision. The reason he needs a liberal education is that he is a man and a citizen, and the major premise of this book is that every man and every free citizen needs liberal education. The prospective research worker also needs it in order to understand his subject. If research is to continue to be the collection of data and the prosecution of experiments in smaller and smaller fields, at some point the research worker is likely to get lost unless he can see where his work fits into some comprehensible whole.

I must say that I think research in this country is an example of the confusion of names and things. No university can now be called respectable that is not respectable in research. Fifty years ago it was just the other way round. Universities were then colleges of liberal arts with professional schools attached. The campaign for research as the distinguishing characteristic of the university was not won until yesterday. The success of the campaign has in large part been the result of snobbishness. Good teaching, however impressive it may be to those who come under it, can enjoy only an esoteric fame. Research can be published, and scientific research can lead to sensational publicity and sometimes to practical results.

But the kind of work that is appropriate to a university must be determined by the nature and purpose of the institution. The kind of research that in my view is most appropriate to a university would not in most universities be called research at all. If research is thinking about important problems, then it seems to me an indispensable part of the work of a university. If research does not involve thinking, as I believe a great deal that is called research does not, then it has no place in a university.

I would not have you think that I believe that anything should be done in a university if only it is useless. There have been epochs in history at which this has been a popular view. Those who would deplore a program for the theological student in how to preach or lead the choir have sometimes seemed to feel that he might labor in the odor of sanctity by writing a dissertation on the life-history of an obscure Scottish divine. The criterion for inclusion or exclusion of subjects in the university cannot, however, be immediate practical usefulness or uselessness. In the example I have given, neither subject should have any place in the university, because neither requires any thought. Thought is hard work, but not all hard work is thought.

The reputation that research or scholarship as it is generally understood has achieved in American universities does not appear to be justified by the purpose of the university. Painful, detailed work on the accumulation of information on trivial subjects may be good for the character. Painful, detailed accumulation of information on any subject may be good for society. Some day somebody might need it. But if it is hard work, or if it is good for society to get all the facts about the origins of the place names in Arthurian romance or about the duties of the Third Assistant Deputy Postmaster-General, it has still not been established that this work should be conducted in a university. To paraphrase Sir Richard Livingstone, "The sign of a good university is the number of subjects that it declines to investigate."

There is every reason to insist that every member of a university community should keep on thinking, but there is none to demand that he conduct research that does not require thought. One aim of a university is certainly to add to the sum of human knowledge. But there is a great difference between knowledge and information. Knowledge is organized information, that is, information that has been reflected upon, thought about. The collection of information for the purpose of thinking about it is a legitimate function of a member of a university, but only on the assumption that he goes on to think about what he collects.

The first question we must ask about activity conducted in the educational system is: Has it intellectual content, and has it such content in its own right? If the activity has no intellectual content, it does not belong in education. If it has intellectual content, but not in its own right, it should be carried on under the auspices of those departments or schools where the intellectual content is properly located.

For example, journalism as such has no intellectual content in its own right. It is an occupation that demands intellectual training and intellectual power. These qualifications may be obtained, in so far as an educational program can supply them, in a good college of liberal arts. I estimate that 85 per cent of the curriculum in schools of journalism is an inadequate imitation of the program in liberal arts and that the balance is technical training in the practices of journalism, which is an inadequate imitation of the training that could be acquired by working on a newspaper.

When we come to those professions which have intellectual content in their own right, like medicine, theology, and law, we see that, if those who enter them do not have a liberal education and an understanding of the intellectual content of the professional discipline, they are no better off than the man on the assembly line whose education consists of vocational training. The lawyer, for example, who is without liberal education and whose legal training consists of exercises in the manipulation of the rules, without any understanding of legal history, jurisprudence, or comparative law, may prove a menace to society and a burden to himself. I need not tell you that in this country the three subjects in which law students receive the least instruction are legal history, jurisprudence, and comparative law. The public does not trust the bar and wants as much of a young lawyer's preparation as possible given under the auspices of the university. The bar is glad to accept this arrangement, because it would like to have its hands as fully trained as possible when they come to work.

It is hard to master the intellectual content of a profession while one is practicing it. The demands of active professional life are not favorable to study and reflection. On the other hand, universities are not well adapted to teaching the tricks of trades. And it is unwise for them to make the attempt. The great problem of the university is the problem of purpose. What is it for? If it undertakes to teach the tricks of some trades, why should it not be willing to assume the same responsibility with regard to any? But why should it try? Unless its professors are engaged in the practice of the occupation, they are unlikely to be adept at the latest tricks; and, if they are actively engaged in the occupation, they are unlikely to be good professors. This is not because of any defect in their character but because the demands of active professional life do not allow them time for study and reflection.

The best division of responsibility between the university and the occupation would be to have the university deal with the intellectual content of the occupation, if there is any, and to have the occupation itself take charge of familiarizing its own neophytes with the technical operations they have to learn. In a long career in university administration, I have never heard anybody advance a single reason why the universities should be charged with the duty of teaching the prospective members of any occupation the techniques of that occupation.

As I have suggested, the basic question in any practical activity, like education, is that of purpose. A purpose is a principle of distribution: it shows you where your efforts should be placed. It is also a principle of limitation: it shows you what you should not do. The purpose of the educational system can be most readily got at by a process of elimination. What would be lost if the educational system were abolished? The loss to the community and to the citizens who compose it would be the loss of an institution dedicated to the intellectual development of the population. Only the educational system can have this aim. Only the educational system can achieve it. If the purpose of the educational system is the intellectual development of the people, then the efforts of the system should be primarily, if not exclusively, devoted to accomplishing this purpose. Since a purpose is a principle of limitation, the efforts of the educational system should be confined to the attempt to promote the intellectual development of the people.

The university rests on the assumption that there should be somewhere in the state an organization the purpose of which is to think most profoundly about the most important intellectual issues. Its purpose is to illuminate the whole educational system and the speculative and practical issues that confront speculative thinkers and men of action. It is a community that thinks.

Extreme and premature specialization in the United States has carried the educational system into activities that have no connection with the intellectual development of the population and has caused a disproportionate amount of its effort to go into such activities. The social and political community that might result from a common understanding has no chance to emerge. Boys and girls are mistrained in specialties and not educated to comprehend the duties of citizenship or the methods by which they might hope to lead happy and useful lives.

The American university, which seems to be concerned almost exclusively with money, and hence with public relations, which are supposed to produce gifts, legislative grants, and tuition income, will offer any course of study that seems likely to interest any influential group in the community; for what standard other than money or public relations can it invoke? I discern the love of money at the bottom of the disintegration of the American university.

Even in Utopia, where the love of money is un-

known, the University confronts the problem of
excessive and premature specialization, because even
in that fortunate country the nature of knowledge
requires specialization. The Utopians limit their professional schools to those occupations which have
intellectual content and have it in their own right.
They leave training in the techniques of professions
to the professions themselves. They believe that nothing can be called a profession unless the members
of the occupation are dedicated to the common good,
unless they have long since forgotten the doctrine of
caveat emptor, and unless they pursue the common
good through their profession instead of merely trying to make a dollar, however honest, through it.
Utopia is something like Wisconsin sixty years ago,
when an old lawyer said to a young lawyer from
New York, "Tell me, is it true what I hear—that
there are men in New York who are practicing law
for money?"

But still the Utopians confront the problem of
specialization because they are dealing in the University with modern knowledge. They feel the influence of science just as much as we do, and they are
quite as good at it as we. The Utopian methods of
meeting the extremes of specialization induced by
science are interesting and instructive. In the first
place, they are not confused about knowledge, and
hence not about research. They do not believe that
the collection of data about insignificant subjects has
any place in a university, and they do not accord high
honors to the collection of data about significant subjects, regarding those honors as properly bestowed

on those who think best about the most significant subjects.

In the second place, the Utopians are not confused by the suggestion that science is the whole of knowledge. They treasure the insights of historians, artists, philosophers, and theologians and insist that, if we are to understand the world and ourselves, we shall need all the light that these insights can give us. Since they are not confused about names and things, they do not say that anything that goes on in a department in the Humanities Division must be humanistic, any more than they would say that an American liberal arts college had much to do with the liberal arts. They do not want the departments in the Humanities Division to be "scientific"; they want them by methods appropriate to their own disciplines to arrive at knowledge. They would recognize that many activities of many departments in the humanities in the United States are now not as humanistic as many activities in many departments called scientific, just as there is today more liberal artistry in some engineering courses than there is in some colleges of liberal arts.

Third, the Utopians recognize that, in order to have a community that thinks, you have to have mutual intelligibility. Society requires specialists; but even specialism requires, if it is not to come to a dead end, that every specialty be able to throw light on every other. Every specialist must therefore be able to catch whatever light is being thrown from any quarter. As a man, as a citizen, and even as a specialist, the specialist requires liberal education. And since even the best liberal education cannot survive the kind of graduate training that most specialists now receive, the Utopians treat graduate education, training for their higher degrees, as principally designed to give the student an understanding of his special field in relation to others. Unless a man is going to be a research worker, they do not set him at research. If he is going to be a teacher, they try to see to it that he understands the subjects that he is likely to teach. If he is going to be a professional man—and professions among the Utopians are very few—they try to make sure that he acquires a knowledge of the intellectual content and the intellectual history of the professional discipline.

Finally, the Utopians have mitigated the worst effects of specialization through the organization of their university. They do not think it enough to have professors and students combined into departments, or even into groups of departments, such as the Sciences, the Humanities, or the Social Sciences. They realize that all such combinations can do is to assist a chemist to speak to another chemist and occasionally to a physicist. In Utopia the object is to make it possible, and even necessary, for everybody to communicate with everybody else. Therefore the University of Utopia is arranged so as to force, in a polite way, the association of representatives of all fields of learning with one another. The University of Utopia is divided into institutions with faculties numbering about twenty-five and students about two hundred and fifty. Each faculty and each student group contain representatives of the major fields.

The work of these institutions rests on that of the College, which in Utopia begins, of course, with the junior year in high school and ends with the sophomore year of the conventional American college. The object of the College of Utopia is to see to it that everybody in it gets a liberal education. One object of the University of Utopia is to see to it that he does not lose it when he has got it. Instead, he is expected to continue and develop it. The result of the combination of a college of this sort and a university organized in this way is that Utopia has been able to take specialization in its stride, to gain the advantages that it has to offer, without suffering the destructive effects that it has brought with it everywhere else in the world.

The organization of the University of Utopia was once like that of an American university. The present organization was, I am told, suggested to the people of that interesting country by a former president of the University, who was tricked into assuming office late in life, after a distinguished career in nuclear physics. Having devoted himself for many years to intellectual activity, which he regarded as identical with life itself, he found that his presidential duties left him no time to think and, of course, no time to teach or carry on research, even of the most pedestrian kind. He thought it odd that the only person in the University who was not required to be a teacher, scholar, or thinker was the head of it. He saw that one of the most unfortunate consequences of specialization was the production of the specialized educational administrator. When he came to retire, therefore, he recommended the organization of the University that I have described in order, among other things, to make the idea of specialized educational administration so absurd that it could never be brought forward again. The head of an institution of twenty-five professors and two hundred and fifty students obviously could not claim that his administrative duties left him no chance to do the kind of work for which the University was established. For this far-sighted act, by which he at once overcame the worst excesses of specialization among his faculty and students and saved his successors from a life of shame, the president of whom I have spoken is lovingly enshrined in the memory of a grateful country.

You will notice that the Utopian educational system and the University of Utopia are highly specialized institutions. What we want is specialized institutions and unspecialized men.[1] We want men who even though they are specialists are still men and citizens and who would ideally be able to move from one specialty to another as their interests and the needs of the community might recommend. We want men who are men and not machines. We must not be misled by the objection that there is now so much to be known that nobody can know enough to understand more than a fragment of a small field. This is to confuse information and knowledge. What every human being needs is a grasp of fundamental ideas and the ability to communicate with others.

On the other hand, we want specialized institutions.

1. This distinction was first brought to my attention by Professor Edward Shils in a seminar of the Committee on Social Thought at the University of Chicago under the chairmanship of Professor Colin Clark.

We want institutions constructed and managed to do a specific job. The more clearly that job is defined, the more likely it is to get done. The political party in a totalitarian state, the church in Spain, the American educational system and university, are examples of underspecialized institutions. Because these institutions undertake to do more than they are equipped to do, they fail in everything. The American educational system, for example, now seems likely to become a custodial system, a system for the nonpenal accommodation of the young from the time at which they become a nuisance to their families to the time at which we are ready to have them go to work. When you hear educators talk about how the educational system needs more money in order to do more things, you may suspect that they are not talking about education; they are talking about the extension of the custodial system.

America may require a custodial system for the young. If it does, that system should be called by its right name and should be appraised in the right terms. We should not seek to apply educational standards to something that does not pretend to be educational. But I would point out that, if through the process of underspecialization the American educational system becomes custodial, America will then be without an educational system. Such a country is without any means for the intellectual development of its population. If the family and the church undertake this responsibility, they will in their turn become underspecialized institutions. They will fail in the educational task and also in the tasks proper to them. A country that makes no effective provision for the intellectual development of its population is headed for dictatorship or worse. A country that makes no provision for serious higher learning, such as the University of Utopia provides, will suffer from the degradation of its culture, the confusion of its thinkers, and the ultimate cessation of its scientific progress.

In the United States, because of the absence of an educational tradition that is widely understood, the universities supported by taxes look more and more like parts of a custodial system. The hope is found in the independent, endowed universities. Here money and public relations are already prime objects of attention; and it may be that the independent universities will become custodial, too. But this will mean only that they have decided to become like everybody else, that the lure of normalcy has been too much for them, and that they have not the courage to be different. In this case they will have ceased to be universities, and they will have ceased to be independent. May Heaven avert the omen and give us the University of Utopia in our own country in our own time.

III

PHILOSOPHICAL DIVERSITY

THE problem raised by philosophical diversity is essentially the same as that produced by specialization. It is the problem of forming a community in the absence of communication. In the educational system, and particularly in the university, it is the problem of forming a thinking community when the members of the community cannot think together because they cannot communicate with one another. Specialization means that specialized men cannot think together because their training and their work have split them off from other men. Philosophical diversity may mean that men cannot think together because their principles, or their underlying assumptions, tacit or expressed, are so different that their conversation, if they try to have any, moves on parallel lines.

This problem is peculiarly difficult because philosophy is itself a university department and is itself highly specialized. Since philosophy is a university department, it cannot be the concern of any other part of the university. We all know that only the English Department can do anything about the kind of writing done by the students in a university. It would be presumptuous for the History Department to set any literary standards for the students in that department, just as it is generally thought impertinent for the English Department to pretend to know anything about history. I shall always treasure the remark of a chairman of the Mathematics Department at the University of Chicago, now long since gone to his reward. He was discussing the future of one of his most promising graduate students, a man of the highest mathematical ability. He said, "You know, I think he's crazy." In some alarm I asked why. The chairman replied, "Why, he is interested in philosophy."

If this was the situation in mathematics, you may imagine what I have seen happen when young men in science or in medicine have exhibited the same strange tendency to begin to wonder about the fundamental presuppositions of their work.

As a university department philosophy is subject to all the other influences affecting university departments, such as the awe universally aroused by experimental science, the misconception of research, and the horrid fate that has overtaken the once-proud degree of Doctor of Philosophy. The specialized department of philosophy often appears to be nonhumanistic, or even antihumanistic, nonintellectual, or even anti-intellectual, engaged in the manufacture by esoteric means of Ph.D.'s who will teach in other departments of philosophy and whose work cannot possibly be of interest to anybody but persons teaching in departments of philosophy.

Things are no better outside the university than within, though which is cause and which effect I do not pretend to know. In a world gone mad over technology, science, the production of material goods,

and lengthening human life it is not to be expected
that the enlightenment that philosophy might provide would be greatly sought after or highly valued.
Nor can I claim that all modern philosophies seem
at first glance capable of shedding much light. Pragmatism and positivism provide no standard for the
criticism of thought; pragmatism provides, perhaps,
a criterion of action. Positivism does not even do
that. In its logical or mathematical manifestations it
seems to be the efflorescence of man's despair that he
cannot more easily make intelligible statements about
the world. Marxism has, of course, an explanation
for everything, but, entirely aside from its vulnera-
bility as the official dogma of a political order that is
repulsive to us, Marxism fails to account in a rational
way for so many important facts about man that it
is hard to take its philosophical pretensions seriously.

The prevailing positivism and scientism assure us
that only the verifiable facts, preferably those veri-
fied in the laboratory, can be in any real sense known
to us. Since man's terrestrial salvation depends on
knowledge, we can look only to the verifiable facts to
save us. Positivism and scientism regard themselves
as completing the task begun by Epicurus and Lu-
cretius two thousand years ago, the task of ridding
mankind of its superstitions.

Since the work of many professional philosophers
is inapplicable to any of the problems of daily life,
and since the work of many is directed to showing
that no philosophy can have any but a harmful effect
on daily life, and since all philosophers seem to disagree anyway, it is natural that the world has steadily

become more and more unphilosophical or antiphilosophical. Why worry about something as vague, useless, confusing, contradictory, and menacing as philosophy seems to be?

Yet civilization is the deliberate pursuit of a common ideal. Education is the deliberate attempt to form men in terms of an ideal. It is the attempt of a society to produce the type of man that it wants. How does it determine the type of man that it wants? If it does not know the type of man that it wants, how does it judge the educational efforts it makes? It may be said that the type of man a society wants is the product of many historical and psychological factors and that whatever philosophy enters into the formation of its vision of man is simply a rationalization of this largely unconscious product. But, even if this were so, we know that in every society there is some vision of man, his nature and his destiny, elaborated by philosophers living and dead, which interacts with the traditional view of the type of man desired and which amounts to a criticism of the tradition and the practices of the educational system. Education without a philosophy of education, that is, a coherent statement of the aims and possibilities of education, is impossible.

Of course a custodial system is possible without a philosophy of education or any other kind of philosophy. A custodial system may be regarded as the efflorescence of a society's despair that it can make no rational and coherent statement about the type of man that it wants to produce. It therefore decides to leave the matter to chance, providing harmless accommodation and occupation for the young until they reach maturity. This, I should be careful to point out, is an entirely different thing from saying that the kind of man we want is one who can think and act for himself and that therefore we are going to let him learn for himself while the educational system does little more for him than keep him out of harm's way.

Though I do not favor this philosophy of education, I admit that it is one. It is an adaptation of the laissez faire or free-enterprise system to education that approaches that popular at Harvard until the retirement of President Eliot. Vestiges of this philosophy still remain to plague the universities; and some versions of Progressive Education seem to be built on the same premises. The two most obvious disadvantages of it are, first, that it implies that teachers need not know, any more than their pupils, what an education is and, second, that it breaks up the community of learning that might exist among students and deprives them of the assistance of their fellow-students and of the ability to communicate with them during their schooling and with their fellow-men in later life.

A custodial system of that frank and open kind which American education seems bent on developing requires neither philosophy nor educational philosophy. The question is whether the philosophical diversity now rampant in the world leads inevitably to a custodial system. Must we say that because philosophers differ, and some even hold that there is no such thing as philosophy, we cannot have a philosophy of education, and hence not an educational system? I assume that we would like to have an educational system, rather than a custodial one, if we could.

If we are to have a philosophy of education, it has to rest on a rational conception of man and society. It also has to take into account the philosophical diversity characteristic of our time. It has to take account, moreover, of the fact that there is no authority that can decide among competing philosophies. The incredible number of school boards, legislatures, boards of regents, boards of trustees, together with principals, superintendents, presidents, chancellors, and faculties, are all more or less autonomous centers of educational decision. The business of raising ourselves by our own bootstraps into a new and rational world will not be easy.

Let us see what we can learn from Utopia. Utopia is singularly like the United States in that there is no central educational authority. Nevertheless, it has been able to develop a philosophy of education. It has been able to do this in spite of the fact that in Utopia, too, there is philosophical diversity. The Utopians even insist that philosophical diversity is a good thing. They say that it has always existed, even in those periods of history in which there has been a strong religious or political authority that nominally exercised control over the thoughts of men. The Utopians point out that such authorities have never succeeded in suppressing, and have usually not tried to suppress, philosophical diversity. The attempt to suppress such diversity has been a manifestation of modern progress and has appeared only with the totalitarian state.

Of course there are in Utopia no underspecialized institutions. The Utopians have never allowed themselves to be annoyed by such slogans as adjustment to the environment or meeting immediate needs, because they have sharply defined the purpose of their educational system. It is to promote the intellectual development of the people. The reason for the strength of the Utopian family and the Utopian church and the Utopian educational system is that each has its prescribed task. No Utopian, for example, would ever have been guilty of the proposition advanced to me the other day by an eminent bishop, who said that education should be limited to the élite and that the mass of the people should receive such culture as they need from the family and the church. The Utopians think that intellectual development is too important to be left to amateurs; and, since they are devoted to democracy, they do not see how they can maintain and improve their democracy unless every citizen has the chance to become as wise as he can.

The Utopians are sensible people. They have sense enough to know that children at the age of six cannot and should not do the kind of work in school that full-grown men should tackle. The Utopians know that physical and moral development are involved in intellectual development. Their educational system makes provision for the participation of educators in physical and moral development at the proper stages and in the proper ways, but never in such ways as to confuse anybody about who has the responsibility at every stage for intellectual development and who for moral and physical growth.

The Utopians believe that education is a conversation aimed at truth. Their object is to get everybody to take part in this conversation. They therefore start their children off by teaching them the techniques of communication. Those of you who have children may feel that this is a work of supererogation; but the Utopians think there is a great difference between chattering and conversing. The first ten years of the Utopian educational system is devoted primarily to reading, writing, and figuring. Because the Utopians are aware of the axiom that subjects that cannot be understood without experience should not be taught to those who are without experience, they do not bother inexperienced children with what are called the social studies. They want to fill their minds and touch their imaginations with the kind of knowledge suitable to their years. In the first ten years of his education, therefore, the young Utopian studies history, geography, and the greatest literature of the world. It is not supposed that he will understand all the implications of history and literature, but it is believed that he should be introduced to them in childhood and in such a way that he will want to continue to study them all his life. Since no one can understand his own language, or what a language is, by speaking or studying his own, every young Utopian masters a foreign language. And every young Utopian studies science;

for this subject the Utopians regard as indispensable to understanding the modern world, and they believe that, as a subject that does not require experience, it is one that children can begin to study very early. In view of the celebrity that Utopians have achieved in the world of art and music, I need hardly add that all of them study these subjects.

By the age of sixteen the young Utopian has studied very few subjects; but he has studied all those appropriate to his time of life. The object has been to get him to go on studying them as long as he lives. The object has also been to fit him to understand any new idea or any new field that presents itself to him. And the great overruling object has been to prepare him to become a member of the republic of learning and of the political republic. Almost all the teaching in Utopia is conducted through discussion. The educational system is a paradigm of the conversation through which learning is advanced and through which a democracy works.

At the age of sixteen, or earlier if he is ready for it, the Utopian passes into the College. Here he continues to study history, geography, literature, science, music, and art, but the emphasis shifts from learning the techniques of communication to obtaining familiarity with the principal views of the world that men have developed and the leading ideas that have animated mankind. The curriculum from the beginning of the elementary school through the College is completely prescribed for all the students. The Utopians do not believe that any civilized man can omit any of the subjects that are included in the course of study. And they do not doubt that the educational profession is better qualified to say what children should study than the children themselves. The Utopians have heard of the American plan, by which a certain number of courses, whatever they are, finally add up to a degree, but the Utopians are, as I have said, a sensible people, and the credit system has never been introduced among them. This is one of the things that makes the country Utopia.

Somewhere between the ages of eighteen and twenty, or whenever he is ready, the Utopian presents himself for examinations that cover the whole of his education up to that point. These examinations, which are constructed by an outside board, reflect what the educational profession of Utopia thinks of as a liberal education, the education appropriate to free men. If the student passes these examinations, he is awarded the degree of Bachelor of Arts. The Utopians have never been confused about the award of this degree at this stage, because the degree has never been debased into a certificate of time served, or credits accumulated, or a license to enter a graduate school, or a qualification for membership in the University Club. It has always stood for liberal education, and this is what the examinations at the end of the College of Utopia stand for, too.

After leaving the College, the young Utopian has two courses open to him. He may enter upon the task of earning his living in the justly famous free-enterprise system of his country, or he may, if he is qualified, proceed to the University. But it never occurs to any Utopian that his education should stop when he leaves college. I have said that one of the premises upon which the educational program of Utopia is constructed is that subjects that cannot be understood without experience should not be taught to the inexperienced. History and literature are taught only by way of introduction in the schools and college of Utopia. The social sciences do not appear as such at all. Yet the Utopians recognize that history, literature, and such knowledge as the social sciences have gained must be understood by civilized men. The Utopians also believe that a man must go on learning all his life, that he can do so if he is a man, and that, if he does not do so, he will cease to be one.

Therefore the whole country is dotted with centers of education for adults young and old, where the most important theoretical and practical questions are discussed. Some of these groups begin with the current issue of the *Utopian Times* and work backward to first principles. Some of them begin with Homer, who enjoys a considerable reputation in Utopia, and work forward to the pressing problems of the day. The object of these groups is not to confer social prestige or vocational advancement upon the members. It is to continue the intellectual development, the liberal education, of the individual as a Utopian and a man.

The centers of adult education in Utopia are all residential. The Utopians have learned that the educational consequences of evening classes scattered over a period of weeks, though they are better than nothing at all, do not compare with those which can be achieved by having groups live together for a limited time and share in that continuous conversation about important subjects which to a Utopian is education. The industrial and agricultural life of the country revolves around the obligation that is felt by the whole community to spend some part of each year in organized study of this kind. No Utopian would think of taking a vacation in the American sense of the word, and the summer resorts, and even winter resorts, of that country are really centers of adult education.

The organization of the University of Utopia I have already roughly described. It is constituted of institutions of about twenty-five professors and two hundred and fifty students each. They are exclusively residential, for the same reason that the centers of adult education in Utopia are residential. Specialized study in Utopia begins only with the University. The University is built on the principle that men who must be intensively trained in the specialties must not lose their liberal education or their ability to communicate with other men or their interest in and capacity to understand ideas in any field of learning. All the major fields of learning are therefore represented in the faculties and among the students of the institutions of which the University of Utopia is composed. Because the Utopians recognize that the tendency of specialization is centrifugal and that every precaution must be taken against this tendency, they require the members of these institutions to live together.

The object of the University of Utopia is the clarification and reinterpretation of basic ideas. All ideas that can seriously pretend to be basic are discussed. The Utopians, because of the character of their liberal education, have little difficulty in assessing the pretensions of various ideas. Those ideas which underlie the learned professions are included. Those occupations which do not rest on any intellectual content or which have none in their own right are necessarily excluded; for how could those interested in them take part in the conversation? Persons who are interested only in the accumulation of data about some subject, even a subject of great importance, like the operations of government, or of the economic system, or of protons or proteins, are, unless they are able to think and communicate about the ideas involved in these phenomena, necessarily excluded, too.

The qualifications of the professors of the University of Utopia are strikingly different from those which prevail in the United States. With us the professor must only be eminent, or give promise of attaining eminence, in his field. In Utopia the professor must be eminent, or give promise of attaining eminence, in his field. This is taken as a matter of course. But unless in addition to meeting this requirement he is also willing and able to receive light from other fields and shed light from his own upon the basic problems that the University is discussing, he cannot be appointed. This conclusion follows remorselessly from the conception of a university that the Utopians entertain.

The students of the University of Utopia are not there because they do not want to go to work, or because they want to move a rung or two up the social ladder, or because they want to learn how to get ahead in some ocupation, or because without the civilizing influence of the Dean of Men or the Dean of Women they might turn into juvenile delinquents. The students are there because they have intellectual interests and have shown in the program of liberal education they have passed through that they are capable of developing them. The University is not concerned with the question whether the studies of these students prepare them to carry on some specific activity in later life. Such a question would be incomprehensible to a Utopian. The Utopians have the conviction that intellectual activity and the discussion of the most important theoretical and practical problems is indispensable to a happy life and to the progress, and even the safety, of the state.

The University of Utopia was conceived and established as a center of independent thought. I have said enough to show in what sense it is a center: everybody can and will communicate with everybody else. I have perhaps said enough to suggest in what sense it deals with thought: anything that is not thought can have no place in it. By this I do not mean that the University is opposed to recreation or social life. The program of extracurriculum activities is startling in its range and richness. All I mean is that the University has never confused these activities with the purpose of the institution. One reason for this is, perhaps, that intercollegiate football has never taken root—it has never even been thought of—in Utopia. As I have said, the Utopians are a sensible people.

Since they are sensible, they do not deny the value of the collection of information or data; nor do they deny the importance of technical training in many fields. And they would be the last to say that a society should not organize itself in some way to bring its knowledge and experience to bear on its urgent practical problems. All that the Utopians claim is that such activities, the collection of data, technical training, and the solution of immediate practical problems, cannot be conducted in a university without disrupting, or at least confusing, the institution. Since they regard the University as a highly specialized institution, they do not want it confused. They see confusion as the first step toward underspecialization and disintegration.

The Utopians understand, however, that men engaged in the collection of data, technical training at high levels, and the solution of urgent practical problems have much to gain from association with a center of independent thought. They also think that the University has much to gain from association with such men and with such undertakings. This is not because the professors are sensitive to the charge that they live in an ivory tower or have never met a payroll—such absurdities are never heard in Utopia—but because the Utopians recognize that anything worth thinking about has consequences in the practical order and that anything in the practical order may suggest something that is worth thinking about.

The Utopians have therefore surrounded the University with organizations collecting data, giving technical training at high levels, and seeking the solution of urgent practical problems, and the interchange between these groups and the members of the University is very active. Neither side of the exchange is at all confused about what is the University and what is not. Neither side would wish to be the other. Each institution is specialized. These arrangements have worked remarkably well. I have heard that they were modeled after those between the Public Administration Clearing House and the University of Chicago.

I have now shown in what sense the University of Utopia is a center and in what sense it is dedicated to thought. In the next chapter I shall attempt to show in what sense it is independent and is therefore entitled to be called a center of independent thought. But I should say something now about the idea of independence as it affects the students of the University.

As you know, they enter the University between the ages of eighteen and twenty, having sought to obtain the beginnings of a liberal education in the College. Their object in the University is to continue this education, to participate in the discussion that is the University, to understand the reasons for things, and to master the ideas in an important field of learning. The first difference that strikes us in looking at what they do and what the American student does lies in the negligible amount of formal instruction given to them. Twenty years ago, when I asked the chairman of the Economics Department at the University of Chicago why he had such large and frequent classes for graduate students, he replied, "Mr. Hutchins, my students cannot learn anything unless I am in the room." When I asked why he didn't get better students, he said, perhaps correctly, that there weren't any.

In Utopia this problem does not arise, because only those students who are qualified to do independent work and who are interested in doing it are admitted to the University. This is, in fact, one of the two great differences between the College and the University. The College does its work through formal instruction, and there is no specialization. In the University formal instruction is at a minimum, and one of the objects of the institution is to advance knowledge in special fields of learning. The College is in session for thirty-six weeks of the year; the University for only twenty-four. Since the Utopians pay no attention to time served as a criterion of intellectual progress, since, of course, there are no accrediting agencies in Utopia to tell the University that only time served can be such a criterion, and since the credit system has never been heard of, the Utopians have no difficulty in concluding that independent study and reflection should constitute the principal activity of the faculty and students of the University. In Utopia the student seldom attends formal class meetings more than four hours a week, and he is not required to attend those.

The method of instruction is chiefly discussion. The professors in the University of Utopia never lecture, except about work that they have in progress. If that work has reached the stage at which it can be written down, it is written down, distributed among the students, and discussed. No Utopian professor would think of giving a course of lectures more than once. To do so would suggest that he had no work in progress or that he was not making any progress with it.

This brief survey of the organization and operation of the Utopian educational system enables us to see in what sense philosophical diversity is a hazard to education and in what sense it may be a positive advantage. Clearly if the educational system is thought of as a means by which society indoctrinates the young with a certain view of life and the world, then philosophical diversity is fatal and must be eliminated, if necessary by the most drastic methods. The drastic methods employed by Nazi Germany and those states which have officially embraced Marxism are known to all of us. If the University is thought of as performing, among other things, the task of training the so-called intelligentsia to preserve, interpret, and teach the official philosophy, then of course philosophical diversity cannot be tolerated. Educational systems and universities in countries that have militant official philosophies may be able to cope with industrialization and specialization by some of the methods practiced in Utopia. But they cannot cope with philosophical diversity. They cannot allow it. They have to take the view that the last word has been said, or at least the last important word, and that to permit the addition of another is to promote error and endanger the unity and safety of the state.

At first glance the problems raised by philosophical diversity in countries that are without an official philosophy seem insoluble. If there are many philosophies, how can we avoid having many educational philosophies? If there are many educational philosophies, how can we avoid having many educational systems, which is manifestly absurd? Yet the Utopian experience may suggest to us that it is possible to have one educational philosophy and many philosophies. The Utopian example may show that a country can have one educational system and one educational philosophy in the face of philosophical diversity.

The Utopians have accomplished this feat by making the consideration of philosophical diversity the primary concern of educational philosophy. A glance at the University of Utopia will show how this is done. The University is not a center of propaganda for an official doctrine. Still less is it an institution like many American universities that is not concerned with doctrine at all. It is concerned with all doctrines that can have any reasonable claim to be taken seriously. Its effort is to work toward a definition of the real points of agreement and disagreement among these doctrines, not in the hope of obtaining unanimity, but in the hope of obtaining clarity. The object is not agreement but communication. The Utopians think it would be very boring to agree with one another. They think it helpful and interesting to understand one another. The University of Utopia, like the educational system as a whole, aims to bring together men of different attitudes, backgrounds, interests, temperaments, and philosophies for the purpose of promoting mutual comprehension. The University of Utopia is an understood diversity.

Thus the educational system of Utopia is a paradigm, or prototype, or model of the republic of learning and the world political republic for which the Utopians yearn. The civilization that the Utopians have established is one in which discussion takes the place of force, and consensus is the basis of action. In theoretical matters the Utopians believe that the continuous refinement of methods and ideas will lead to the development of new ideas and hence to the advancement of knowledge. The Utopians are willing to examine the pretensions of any plan of action or of any theoretical proposition.

But, though they are convinced that philosophical diversity is a good thing, in order to have a university or an educational system at all, they have had to impose some limits on the length and breadth of their philosophical tolerance. These limits can be indicated by reporting the kinds of men who cannot be appointed to the faculty of the University of Utopia. There is the kind of man who believes that he knows everything, who is closely related to, if not identical with, the kind of man who does not want to learn anything. Then there is the kind of man who does not want to talk with anybody. Within these limitations the Utopians are very catholic in their philosophical tastes. The prime question is not the source or character of a man's philosophy, but whether he is willing to discuss it. The nature of liberal education in Utopia, and the universal diffusion of that education, has reduced the number of Utopians who are unwilling or unable to discuss their ideas almost to the vanishing point. The wide differences of view among them in regard to such matters as the nature of man, the purpose of the state, and the existence of God have not prevented them from developing a coherent educational program.

The type of man the Utopians wish to produce through their educational system is, I suppose, clear enough. He is a man who has achieved wisdom through the use of his reason and through experience. The Utopians do not regard education as a substitute for experience, but only as preparation for it. They believe, however, that a trained mind is essential to the comprehension of experience and that the object of the specialized institution called the educational system is to equip the people in this way to deal with the problems that confront them. I should add that, though to American eyes the educational system of Utopia may look impractical, detached from life, and unrealistic, the Utopians have made a remarkable record as they have faced contemporary problems. Industrialization, specialization, and philosophical diversity have not thwarted their efforts to understand the world and themselves. They have had no difficulty in finding their way among conflicting ideologies: after all, the population is trained to criticism.

These triumphs of understanding you might expect, since they are triumphant solutions of intellectual problems. What I am sure will strike you as singular, or even sensational, is the success of the Utopians in dealing with the kind of practical issues that seem beyond resolution in the West today. This is the place to emphasize that the Utopian educational system as a whole, and the University of Utopia in particular, are in constant touch with the life of the people and constantly seeking to illuminate the practical problems that the people confront. The great difference between the American university and the University of Utopia on this point is that Utopian educators never lose sight of what the University is for and never confuse the contribution they can make to the solution of a practical problem with that which can be made by industrialists, bankers, and politicians. The object of the University of Utopia is not to mirror the chaos of the world but to straighten it out.

For example, the press, radio, and television of Utopia are renowned for the accuracy of their reports and the illumination that they shed on what is going on. These instruments of communication are regarded as a contribution to the informal education of Utopian adults. They are thought of as a means of public enlightenment. How are these results achieved? Not through schools of journalism. The men who manage and write for what are called the media of mass communication in Utopia receive an education in the College and, if they wish, in the University. They learn their trade in the practice of it. Their education has equipped them to read and write, to think about important questions, and to discuss them intelligently. This is one part of the story. The rest is found in the training of the people with whom they communicate. The Utopians are a people trained to criticism. Since the hoopla of propagandists and advertising men would leave them unmoved, there is no point in indulging in it. At last reports there were no propagandists or advertising men in that happy country.

As I conclude this necessarily brief and incomplete account of the organization and activities of the educational system of Utopia, I must do my best to answer a question that I am sure is in your minds. You may grant that the Utopians have found a way to meet the educational hazards of industrialization, specialization, and philosophical diversity, but you may feel that the cures they have invented are worse than the diseases. Granted that the talk in Utopia is about the most important subjects, granted that communication is indispensable to a community, that every social group should be a community, and that a university should be a thinking community, when do these people decide anything, and when and how do they learn to do it? How do they ever get any convictions? Have they any? Can an ideal country be one in which people are forever talking and communicating and trying to find out what they ought to think and believe? Isn't it possible, in short, to carry this sort of thing too far?

If I may say so, the questions that I have attributed to you, perhaps falsely, reveal what is wrong with the world today rather than what is wrong with Utopia. The Utopians distinguish sharply between knowledge and opinion. They also distinguish sharply between two methods of advancing knowledge: the method of discussion and the method of discovery.

The Utopians have nothing but praise for the scientific method; they are experts at it. Because they are experts at it, they recognize its limitations. They use it to advance knowledge about the world and man. They do not think that it is the only way of advancing knowledge. The Utopians note with interest, but without surprise, that most of the things they know were not learned by this method, because they knew them before this method was much practiced or much regarded. They came to know by the method of discussion the things they knew before the method of discovery was in common use. The Utopians do not believe that the method of discovery has supplanted the method of discussion. They insist that they need both, employing each in the fields in which each is appropriate. Therefore they do not say, for example, that they can learn only in the laboratory, because no knowledge can be obtained outside it. They say they learn the things that can be learned in the laboratory by the method of discovery and the things that can be learned outside it by the method of discussion.

When the Utopians enter upon the discussion of a matter, they ask themselves what kind of matter it is. Is it one about which they can hope to obtain knowledge, or is it one on which with the best will in the world and the most careful thinking the results can be merely probable? If it is one on which reasonable men can agree that knowledge should be obtainable, the Utopians inquire whether they can arrive at knowledge by discussion of the subject. If they can, they go to work on it with knowledge as the end in view. If it is a matter on which it is clear that reasonable men can always differ, if, in short, it is a matter of opinion, such as the precise reasons for the defeat of Napoleon at Waterloo, the Utopians discuss it and investigate it with a view to arriving at the most enlightened opinion. If it is a matter for action, such as whether the Utopians should negotiate with the Philistines, the Utopians deliberate with a view to the most enlightened decision.

There are two reasons why the discussions conducted in Utopia have had such inspiring results in the material, intellectual, and political progress of the country. First, the Utopians know what they are talking about. They do not say that everything is a matter of opinion, and one man's opinion is as good as any other man's. This would mean either that no discussion took place, on the ground that it was useless; or that the discussion was endless. The Utopians say that knowledge in certain fields can be advanced by discussion. As to matters of knowledge, the Utopians intend to arrive at the truth by the method of discussion, in so far as the subject is one the knowledge of which is susceptible of advancement by this method. As to matters of opinion, the Utopians hope to reach the most intelligent conclusion, whether theoretical or practical.

The second reason why the discussions in Utopia have the high quality that distinguishes them is that the Utopians have convictions. They have convictions because they think. Their whole educational program is designed to force them to do so from their youth up. They submit their convictions to the scrutiny of their fellows in the expectation that through the consideration and comparison of the reasons for their convictions knowledge or right opinion, as the case may be, will ultimately be attained.

What is in other countries a serious hazard to education, philosophical diversity, turns out to be in Utopia an educational advantage. This is because of the way in which the educational system and the University are organized and managed. We shall see in the next chapter whether the theory and practice of education in Utopia throw any light on ways to overcome what is perhaps the greatest of all hazards to education in the United States today—the powerful drive toward social and political conformity.

IV

SOCIAL AND POLITICAL
CONFORMITY

THE universities from which our own are descended were founded in the Middle Ages. They were either corporations of students wanting to learn, as in Italy, or of teachers wanting to teach, as in France. Corporations that had unusual legal or customary privileges for the purpose of carrying out the intentions of the incorporators were common in those days. In some Italian cities the Guelf and Ghibelline party clubs, sworn to subvert the state, were recognized corporations specially licensed to work on the project they had in view. The university corporations of the Middle Ages at the height of their power were not responsible to anybody, in the sense that they could not be brought to book by any authority. They claimed, and succeeded in making their claim good, complete independence of all secular and religious control.

In asserting and establishing this claim, they had one inestimable advantage: they had no property. If any secular or religious authority sought to control them, they would simply move away. Since the language that they used was good in any country, since a university was welcome anywhere, and since an inclination to travel has always been characteristic of the academic profession, they had no difficulty in translating themselves to another community or country whenever they felt the atmosphere of the one they were in was oppressive.

For example, the natural enemy of the University of Bologna, which was a corporation of students wanting to learn, was the landladies. When they put the rents too high, the students would move the University out of town and wait until a delegation of landladies besought them, with suitable tears, to return and fixed a scale of prices acceptable to the student-managers of the University. The University of Paris several times thwarted the attempts of king or archbishop to control it by leaving the city or threatening to do so.

All the medieval universities that amounted to anything were of the same general type. They were formed because somebody wanted to learn or somebody wanted to teach. They maintained their independence on the ground that it was necessary to the performance of their corporate function. They did not regard themselves as servants of either church or state. They thought of themselves as co-ordinate with both. The exceptions, like the University of Naples, which fell early under the control of the king, played no significant role in the history of medieval thought. Although the men produced by the medieval universities became leaders in the church and in the state, they did not advertise that their function was to produce such men. Such men were a by-product of the enterprise in which they were engaged, which was singularly like the enterprise of the University of Utopia: it was the discussion of the most important questions. They would have been startled if they had been asked to justify their existence in terms of the service they performed for society, for they would have had no doubt that the discussion they were carrying on was its own justification.

Only faint traces of these origins can be found in the organization and management of the American universities. Every American university must justify itself in terms of the visible, tangible, material benefits that it confers upon the individuals who attend it and the community that supports it. To Americans universities are businesses like every other element of this business civilization. Every business consists of employers and employees. The trustees or regents or legislatures are the employers. The professors are employees. They operate within the framework of the American Way of Life and are subject to punishment for deviation from the popular view of that Way like any other members of the business community. Academic freedom is, I think, generally regarded as a device by which weak-minded or vicious people in some way hang on to their jobs when all right-thinking men would agree that they ought to lose them.

The current conception of the university seems to have its roots deep in our history. The American university was not a corporation of students wanting to learn or teachers wanting to teach. It was a corporation formed by a religious denomination or by the state for the purposes of the denomination or the state. The American university in the seventeenth century was much closer to the American university today than to the medieval university. The Puritan communities wanted ministers and professional men and established universities as a means of getting them. Later the religious groups wanted to extend their influence and built universities for that purpose. The University of Chicago was founded by devout Baptists to stem the rising tide of Methodism in the Middle West. The requirements as to the religious affiliations of the president and the trustees were designed to keep the University on the right path. Fortunately, the combination of Mr. Rockefeller, Mr. Harper, and the enlightened wing of the Baptist Church preserved the University from too narrow an interpretation of its purpose.

Thomas Jefferson took peculiar pride in the fact that he was the founder of the University of Virginia. He was, of all the great men in American history, the most enlightened about the purposes of education. But he wrote a resolution of the Board of Visitors of the University that could never have been written in any other country. Perhaps I should point out that a board of visitors would not have existed in any other country. The board of trustees is an American invention and one that goes far to suggest the different conception of a university that America originated. A corporation of students or a corporation of teachers does not need a board of owners composed of outsiders. A university that is founded to serve the purposes of the state, or of a religious denomination, or of any other external group will naturally be owned and operated by the representatives of the agency that established it.

This was Thomas Jefferson's resolution: "Whereas,

it is the duty of this Board to the government under which it lives, and especially to that of which this university is the immediate creation to pay especial attention to the principles of government which shall be inculcated therein, and to provide that none shall be inculcated which are incompatible with those on which the Constitution of this State, and of the United States were genuinely based, in the common opinion; . . . Resolved, that it is the opinion of this Board that as to the general principles of liberty and the rights of man, in nature and in society, the doctrines of Locke, in his 'Essay concerning the true original extent and end of civil government,' and of Sidney in his 'Discourses on government,' may be considered as those generally approved by our fellow citizens of this, and the United States, and that on the distinctive principles of the government of our State, and of that of the United States, the best guides are to be found in, 1. The Declaration of Independence, as the fundamental act of union of these States. 2. The book known by the title of 'The Federalist,' being an authority to which appeal is habitually made by all, and rarely declined or denied by any as evidence of the general opinion of those who framed, and of those who accepted the Constitution of the United States, on questions as to its genuine meaning. 3. The Resolutions of the General Assembly of Virginia in 1799 on the subject of the alien and sedition laws, which appeared to accord with the predominant sense of the people of the United States. 4. The valedictory address of President Washington, as conveying political lessons of peculiar value. And that in the branch of the school of law, which is to treat on the subject of civil polity, these shall be used as the text and documents of the school."

Here we have the most enlightened American statesman of his day, and perhaps the most enlightened of any day, writing a resolution by which an outside board, representing the state government, prescribes not only the books that shall be taught but also the meaning that is to be derived from them. The object of the instruction of the University of Virginia in the field of political science is to inculcate those principles upon which the constitutions of the United States and of Virginia were genuinely based. These genuinely basic principles are what common opinion, as interpreted by the author of the resolution, says they are. It is the duty of the Board of Visitors to see to it that these principles are inculcated and that nothing incompatible with these principles is inculcated.

The difficulty of determining from common opinion the principles upon which the constitutions of the United States and of Virginia are genuinely based is revealed by a brief examination of an example that Jefferson uses, the Resolutions of the General Assembly of Virginia in 1799 on the Alien and Sedition Acts. These resolutions, like the Kentucky Resolutions, which were drafted by Jefferson, were in opposition to legislation formally adopted by the Congress of the United States and signed by the President. At the date of these resolutions the constitutionality of this legislation had not been attacked in the courts. The opponents of the Alien and Sedition Acts preferred to rely on the protest they could stir up among the state legislatures. The leading idea of the Virginia and Kentucky resolutions was that the Constitution was a compact between the states and that the states had reserved the right to restrain the creature of the compact, the federal government, whenever it undertook to exercise authority not expressly granted to it in the Constitution.

That this idea was not sufficiently shared to be called the common opinion, or the predominant sense, of the people of the United States is suggested by the history of the Kentucky Resolutions. They were laid before the legislatures of the various states. Replies were received from Connecticut, Delaware, Massachusetts, New Hampshire, New York, Rhode Island, Vermont, and Virginia. All but Virginia said that they did not share the Kentucky opinion of the principle on which the Constitution was genuinely based. And though the common opinion of the people in regard to the Alien and Sedition Acts was eventually shown to be unfavorable, the idea of states rights put forward by Madison and Jefferson in the Virginia and Kentucky resolutions was never the common opinion. Today it is so little the common opinion that if the members of the faculty of the University of Virginia attempted to follow the instructions of their founder they might get into serious trouble. Jefferson in this section of his resolution was trying to make the University of Virginia the mouthpiece of the Republican party in its fight with the Federalists.

Since there is this exalted precedent for the attempt

to make the American university a means of indoctrination in the common opinion, or even indoctrination in a partisan view of what the common opinion ought to be, it is not surprising that in religious, economic, and political controversy one side or another has often tried to take over the university. The outstanding example in more recent times was the free-silver fight, in which presidents and professors lost their jobs because they took a view of the issue that was unpopular with those in a position to control the university. If a university is to inculcate doctrines indorsed by common opinion and to shun doctrines not so indorsed, those who seek to teach, or even to express, unpopular doctrines must be disposed of. Academic freedom is thus disposed of, too.

This attitude helps to transform an educational system into a custodial system, and a custodial system tends to confirm this attitude. If one object of a university or of an educational system is to indoctrinate the young with the common opinion, the doctrine of adjustment to the environment becomes one of the cornerstones of pedagogy. The other cornerstone is the doctrine of immediate needs; for it can be argued that one thing the community most immediately needs is citizens who have been indoctrinated with the common opinion. Thus we come to view a university as a place in which the young are familiarized with the tribal mores and in which other activities immediately useful to the community are carried on.

This idea of a university is not helpful in meeting the present criticism of American education ema-

nating from congressional committees, which is to
the effect that persons who do not share the common
opinion as the members of such committees interpret
it are not qualified to teach. We do not care enough
about religion any more to worry about the religious
views of members of university faculties. The Fed-
eralist-Republican and free-silver fights are dead issues. But whereas the Communist experiments in this
country were once regarded as the work of harmless
eccentrics, and ignored as such, now the discovery
that a man has read the works of Karl Marx, or knows
somebody who has, is enough to raise a question
about trusting him in the classroom. Undoubtedly
this attitude results from the Cold War, and when the
Cold War comes to an end, as all things must, the
intensity of the feeling in regard to teachers who are
alleged to hold heretical political or economic views
will somewhat abate. But I suggest that our trouble
is more fundamental than the Cold War, that it rests
on a misconception of education and of the university,
and that, after the present issues disappear, others will
arise to plague us in their turn. Unless we can figure
out what education is and what a university is, and
unless we can build up a tradition in this country that
supports these conceptions, education and the universities will always be at the mercy of those who
honestly or for political purposes seek to make them
the protagonists of their views.

I believe that the educators of America are largely
responsible for the present confusion in and about
education. They have felt obligated in my day to
seek for money, first, last, and all the time. They have

always supposed, I think erroneously, that money could be obtained only for activities that harmonized with the interests and opinions of those who had it. What they have done and what they have not done has been determined by financial considerations. When New York University dropped intercollegiate football the other day, it did not say it was doing so because football in its present big-time, industrial form is an outrageously immoral activity, not only a departure and diversion from the purpose of the university but also directly contrary to it. No, New York University said that it was abandoning football because football lost money.

I admit that this is a business civilization and that businessmen understand profit-and-loss statements and balance sheets. But one of the functions of educational leadership is to explain to businessmen that since a university has no profit-and-loss statement, and since its balance sheet is meaningless, there must be other standards by which its work is judged. Those standards are supplied by its purpose.

In the nature of the case the educators of the country are required to identify the financial needs of their institutions with the moral, intellectual, and spiritual needs of the country. Hence the remarkable confusion of names and things that characterizes American education. Perhaps the most glaring example at present is the colleges of liberal arts. Every American is first asked to admit that he believes in liberal education. Since he believes in liberal education, he must support the colleges of liberal arts. But the question, "How much liberal education is there in the colleges of liberal arts?" is regarded as indecent. Yet about all we can say is that a college of liberal arts is one that does not usually have professional schools. Of course a good many of them have schools of theology, music, and business; but we have to have some kind of definition. The one we emerge with leaves us with this definition of liberal education: liberal education is the name given to what is done in a college that is called a college of liberal arts. The only basis of judging a college of liberal arts today is to inquire whether it does what other colleges of liberal arts do. It is obviously impossible to ask whether any of them ought to be doing what they are doing. The standard of purpose cannot be invoked.

What I have said about colleges of liberal arts applies just as well to the humanities, the social sciences, and, as we have seen, to education itself. If you believe in the humanities—and who does not?— then you must support the work of professors of the humanities, even if they are not doing anything humanistic. If you believe in understanding society, then you must support professors of social science, even those whose work seems unlikely to help us understand society. If you believe in education—how un-American not to do so!—then you must contribute as generously as you can to American educational institutions. And you must do this even though you have reason to suspect that these institutions are rapidly becoming custodial, rather than educational, institutions.

When the Association of American Colleges met

in Los Angeles this winter, the newspapers reported that they spoke of nothing but money and gave the world to understand that, if only they could get enough of it, the country was safe.

What is the use of doubling the expenditures on higher education, as recommended by the President's Commission in 1947, unless it is possible to make sense out of what it is doing? If the system is to be custodial, let us figure out whether we need a custodial system, what a good one would be, and what it would cost. If, in addition, we need an educational system, let us make the same inquiries and calculations in regard to it. But, above all, let us not be confused about which is which. The confusion from which we suffer at present has a good deal to do with the difficulty we encounter in meeting the criticism of congressional committees and in defending academic freedom.

Let us imagine that this country eventually has a well-developed and fully understood custodial system. The object of such a system, you will remember, is to preserve the young from harm while they are maturing. The staff is selected with a view to its performance of this important task. This task is more closely analogous to baby-sitting than to any other in our culture. It may perhaps be called adolescent-sitting.

Let us suppose that the Association of Adolescent-Sitters brings pressure to bear upon custodial institutions arising out of the sense of responsibility (and scarcity) that every adolescent-sitter shares. This pressure is toward security of tenure and freedom of speech, thought, association, within and without the boundaries of the custodial institution in which the particular adolescent-sitter is employed. Certainly it is only confusing the issue if these claims are summarized under the name of academic freedom. An adolescent-sitter who does not indoctrinate his charges as far as he can with the tribal mores and the means of adjusting himself to his environment, who disturbs the young people committed to his care by introducing unfamiliar ideas, who does not seek to meet the immediate needs of those whom he is looking after and of the society of which they are to be a part—such a man merits whatever condemnation the community decides to visit upon him.

The claim of academic freedom is based on the high and serious calling of the academic profession. That calling is to think. A university is a center of independent thought. Since it is a center of thought, and of independent thought, it is also a center of criticism. The freedom of the modern university in a democratic society is based not on the remnants of a medieval tradition but on the proposition that societies require centers of independent thought and criticism if they are to progress or even to survive. Academic freedom means that the independence of the thought that goes on in a university is so important to society that a man cannot be restrained or punished by those who pay him because he holds views with which those who pay him disagree.

To maintain the claim of academic freedom, it is not necessary to prove that all professors can and do think independently. It is enough to show that, unless the freedom claimed for them is guaranteed, it

will be impossible ever to assemble a faculty that ca[n]
and will think. Few men can be expected to expres[s]
unpopular opinions if in addition to becoming un[-]
popular they are likely to starve to death.

I do not say that it is the object of a university t[o]
develop and express unpopular opinions. I do not sa[y]
that the object of a university is to prevent socia[l]
and political conformity rather than promote it. [I]
do say that a university in which no unpopula[r]
opinions are heard or one which merges imperceptibl[y]
into the social and political environment can be pre[-]
sumed, until the contrary is proved, not to be doin[g]
its job. If a university is a center of independen[t]
thought and criticism, then a popular university [is]
a contradiction in terms.

The claim upon the financial resources of the coun[-]
try that a university can legitimately make rests o[n]
the same grounds. Public bodies or private person[s]
who have money to dispense must be asked to do s[o]
not on the promise that the university will produc[e]
a lot of people in their image but on the assurance tha[t]
the university will do its best to carry on the independ[-]
ent thought and criticism that the country require[s]
and to turn out graduates who are capable of independ[-]
ent thought and criticism, graduates, that is, wh[o]
are committed to the fullest development of the[ir]
highest powers and who can do their part as respon[-]
sible citizens of a democratic state.

The greatest obligation of the educational pro[-]
fession and of all those who have the interests o[f]
education at heart is to try to make this conception o[f]
a university clear to their fellow-countrymen. Th[e]

history of education shows that the crucial point in the management of universities is not who has the legal control. Free and independent universities have existed where the control of the state was undoubted. On the other hand, universities established by private groups have been distorted beyond recognition by the pressures that have been brought to bear on them. The crucial point in the management of universities is whether and when the legal control is exercised. This depends on the understanding of the university and its purpose that is held by those who have the legal control and on the understanding of the university and its purpose that is held by the community. It depends, in short, on the tradition within which the university operates. The first duty of the educational profession and of those who have the interests of education at heart is to devote themselves to the development of this tradition. The first step toward the performance of this duty is to exclude from the universities those activities which are not proper to it, which prevent understanding of the function of the universities, and which create confusion in regard to it. The award of college credit at Florida State University for being a clown is as great a disservice to higher education and academic freedom as any of the carryings-on of Senator McCarthy or Congressman Velde.

Unfortunately these gentlemen would have no objection to the clowning program of the Florida State University, because that does not involve thought, still less independent thought and criticism. Like many other Americans, they unconsciously favor a custodial system. This shows the seriousnes of our failure to develop an educational traditior in the United States. It also shows that many of u have a false idea of unity. One gets from some of the statesmen of the day the same impression, that unde the influence of the Cold War they have concludec that a country is not safe unless it is united, whicl is true, and then that a country cannot be united un less everybody in it agrees with everybody else about everything, which is false. The pleas for unity during the last electoral campaign had the same spe cious quality. That civilization of which a true uni versity is a paradigm is one that is based on the prem ise that discussion is one way of arriving at the truth Discussion implies that there is more than one point of view. The notion that the truth may be arrived a by discussion is peculiarly applicable to practical political, economic matters. A civilization in whicl the opinion of the majority is taken on such matter and must then be adopted by all is one that is doomec to stagnation. It ignores the fact that the most pre cious possession of any society is the thought of the minority, even a minority of one. The rule of the majority without discussion and criticism is tyranny

The great new term of reproach nowadays is "controversial." The dream of the public relations man is that all the people of America will discern in his clients the perfect combination of all the popular stereotypes of the day. Hence the tendency toward flat conformity to what the public relations man dis covers, through a series of careful polls, to be the prevalent opinion at the moment. Hence the elimination of men, ideas, books, and opinions that may attract unfavorable notice as differing from the prevalent opinion. In many quarters during the last political campaign a man became controversial by being for Stevenson. Professors who said they were for him were held to endanger the public relations of their universities, though those who were for Eisenhower were of course not controversial at all. I do not think I exaggerate when I say that in a democratic society controversy is an end in itself. A university that is not controversial is not a university. A civilization in which there is not a continuous controversy about important issues, speculative and practical, is on the way to totalitarianism and death.

Such a society may be said to be united, but it cannot be regarded as strong. We do not think it is a sign of strength that the rulers of Russia find it necessary to seek out and punish dissent. On the contrary, we have sense enough to see that the secret police and the Iron Curtain and the universal program of indoctrination practiced in Russia amount to a confession of weakness. The rulers of Russia do not have enough confidence in the adherence of the people to the principles of communism or in those principles themselves to permit a free continuing discussion of them. If we want an example of a strong society, all we have to do is to look at that association of thirteen struggling states which at the outset of its career, as it faced a sea of troubles, adopted the Bill of Rights of our Constitution. The United States of that day may have looked weak and disunited. Actually it was strong because it was not afraid. It was not afraid to have its principles submitted to critical examination. It was united in the conviction that strength and progress lay not in social and political conformity but in the constant exercise of individual judgment, in independent thought and criticism.

Perhaps I should not say that the drive toward social and political conformity that we are witnessing today is un-American. I will say that it is un-Utopian. If there were a House Committee on Un-Utopian Activities, as of course there is not, it would dedicate itself to seeking out and exposing those elements in the community which were trying to put an end to difference and hence to that discussion which the Utopians regard as the essence of true Utopianism. In Utopia the rich and the conservative agree that, looking at matters only in terms of their own selfish interests—something that is hard for a Utopian to do—the preservation of free discussion and criticism is the best guaranty against violent attacks upon Utopian institutions. Because the University of Utopia symbolizes the highest aspirations of Utopian civilization, it naturally receives the support, the almost automatic support, of all classes of society. The only kind of university that could be popular with the Utopians is one in which the most lively controversy was continuously under way. The award for the Most Controversial Person, which is bestowed with great ceremony on the anniversary of the day on which the Utopians declared their independence of the Philistines, is usually won by a professor of the University of Utopia.

In Utopia the public relations men are closely related to the priesthood and are usually called public duty men. Their job is to point out to their clients what their public duty is. The public duty men of Utopia are, together with the lawyers and priests, the conscience of their clients. They show them not how they can look better than they are, but how they can be better than they look. It is assumed that, with the steady advancement of education in Utopia, perfect Utopianism will eventually be achieved and that the class of public duty or public relations men will wither away.

The University of Utopia has men who serve to remind it of its public duty. They are called the Trustees. Their job is not to operate the University but to criticize it. They criticize it in terms of its purpose. They believe that, if it seeks to achieve its purpose, it will not fail to receive public support. The Board of Trustees of the University of Utopia was created by legislation resting on the proposition that every autonomous body of men requires criticism and that it is not usually capable of self-criticism. The Utopians recognize that professors are people. They accord them the usual privileges of people, which is Utopian in itself; but the Utopians know that professors have the ordinary failings of people, the principal one of which is an inability to see beyond their noses where their own interests are involved. The Board of Trustees is a means of keeping the professors up to the mark. In Utopia, of course, the professors are in no sense employees. They are members of the educational corporations constituting the University of Utopia. They manage their own affairs, elect their own colleagues and officers, and determine their own programs of study and research. But they do all this under the constant criticism, public and private, of the Trustees.

One question formerly much agitated in Utopia was what the limits of the discussion permitted to the people and more particularly to the educational system and the University were to be. In answering this question, the Utopians had certain historical advantages. They had never heard of the celebrated dictum of Mr. Justice Holmes about crying fire in a crowded theater or of the remark of Mr. Chief Justice Vinson that freedom of speech was not an absolute, since absolutes were a relic of the Dark Ages. The Utopians approached the matter with their usual common sense. They asked themselves what they were afraid of. They concluded that what they were afraid of was acts. They could not imagine themselves being afraid of ideas, or of talk, or of discussion. They therefore decided that any Utopian could say anything he liked on any subject at any time. They never let poetic imagery carry them away into thinking that this meant that a man could cry fire in a crowded theater, and they did not permit the pseudo-philosophy of even their distinguished judges to delude them into supposing that a principle should be abandoned just when they needed it most.

The Utopians do not like spies and traitors any better than anybody else does. The Utopian Bureau of Investigation is supposed to be competent to discover them; the Utopian House and Senate would be surprised to learn that it was any part of their duty to hunt spies and traitors, too. Spies and traitors are not welcome as teachers in the University of Utopia. But, in view of the efficiency of the Utopian Bureau of Investigation, the University is not expected to devote its energies to the search for spies and traitors among its staff.

The Utopians think that what matters is what the individual man himself is like. They do not deny that a man's tendencies may be suggested by his associations; but they insist that organizations being what they are—Utopia is full of organizations, all of them rather loosely held together by statements of principle that are both voluminous and vague—membership in an organization is of very slight evidential value in showing what a man is really like. If, for example, a man has taught with satisfaction to the University and to his students for twenty years, the fact that he belongs to some organization that has been shown to contain some spies and traitors does not strike the Utopians as very impressive. In Utopia a professor is a citizen and as a citizen may engage in any activity, public or private, in which any other citizen may legally engage. The reason why the law sets the limits of a citizen's conduct is that the Utopians are determined that those limits shall not be set by the shifting prejudices of the time. They see no alternative but the law. The real academic crime is indoctrination, which is only slightly worse in Utopia than the crime of refusing to discuss. For these crimes a Utopian professor can be removed after a hearing by the academic body. I am told that the sentence of removal, followed by the ceremony of disgowning, is often visited upon a Utopian professor for trying to indoctrinate his students with the principles upon which the Utopian Constitution is genuinely based in the common opinion and for failing to cooperate with his colleagues in bringing other interpretations of the Constitution and of the common opinion to the student's attention. The Utopian professor is supposed to have convictions, the deeper the better. He is not supposed to pump and pound them into his students, even though his opinions are shared by the overwhelming majority of the population.

The reason why the University of Utopia is so utopian is that the people of Utopia are utopians. The people want the kind of university they have. The educational tradition in Utopia is such that it would make no difference whether the educational system was operated by the state or by private persons. The educational system is supposed to be a continuing discussion of important subjects. The people want this discussion continued. They see no limits that must be set to discussion. Therefore the question whether the educational system is discussing improper questions does not arise. The only question that arises is whether the discussion is being conducted with sufficient vigor and sufficient representation of different points of view.

I have indicated earlier that the representation that a point of view is entitled to is determined by its intellectual rather than its political pretensions. The point of view of an enemy state is neither included nor ignored because it is the point of view of an enemy state. It is included if it has some intellectual claim to consideration, and it is ignored if it has not. The Utopians believe that a point of view can be presented best by somebody who has it. When the point of view of an enemy state is entitled to intellectual consideration, the Utopians appoint a professor who has the enemy's point of view, if they can find one good enough, to set it forth and participate in the discussion concerning it. This may be one of the reasons why the Utopians have never been taken unawares by the doctrine of an enemy state, as the South was at the time of the American Civil War. At that time the presentation of the northern position by one sympathetic to it had so long been forbidden in the South that the young men of that region gaily went to war in ignorance of the possibility that there was another position that could be seriously entertained, so seriously, indeed, that other people might be willing to lay down their lives for it. The Utopians, as I have said, are disturbed by enemy acts, not by enemy ideas. They want to be as fully informed as possible concerning enemy ideas. They think any other course is folly.

You may wonder how the Utopians, in a world full of dangers, are willing to run the risk of exposing their young people to the ideas of their enemies. How can they be sure that their own young people will not adopt these ideas, particularly if they are expressed by a competent man who holds them and who is entitled to intellectual respect?

As you may have gathered, the essence of the Utopian Way of Life is that it is rational. The Utopians do not think that they know it all. If they can learn from anybody, they want to do so, and they think it particularly intelligent to learn from their enemies. Since nobody who had ever lived in the Utopian atmosphere of freedom would want to live anywhere else, and since the Utopians are perfectly adapted to peaceful change, they are prepared for any change that the discussion of other people's ideas may bring about.

Moreover, the Utopians do not share the prevailing prejudice that the young are so many sheets of blank paper upon which their teachers may write anything they please. Utopian family and religious life is expected to leave, and does leave, its mark upon the young. The concern of the Utopians is not that their young people will be too receptive to new ideas but that the effects of Utopian family and religious life will be so deep that the young will not be at all receptive to new ideas from any quarter.

Finally, remember the tone and content of Utopian education from the kindergarten through the University. The whole object of this system is to train the young Utopian to appraise theories and programs. The Utopians are perfectly willing to abide by the result. A population so trained, and experienced in practical affairs, is as wise as any people can be. The Utopians believe that a wise people will not make unwise choices. If the people in their wisdom want a change, that change, the Utopians believe, is necessary and desirable.

The question is, then, whether it is possible to have the University of Utopia without having Utopians. The answer would seem to be in the negative. Education is a secondary, dependent subject. Yet let us look somewhat more closely into the matter. If we conclude that we cannot have the University of Utopia without having Utopians, we shall be in desperate condition indeed; for how shall we ever get Utopians unless we can produce them through the educational system?

In the first place, just how Utopian does a people have to be in order to establish the educational system and the University of Utopia? Apparently they have to be only this far along the road to Utopia: they have to want to get there. If they want to get there, they will decide that the kind of educational system and the kind of university they want are the kind that Utopia has. These institutions are designed to produce wisdom. A country that wants them needs to want nothing more than to be wise.

History suggests that the other things a country is likely to want are riches and power. It also suggests that riches and power are not enough. At this moment Korea and the atomic bomb provide all the evidence we need. Being rich and powerful is not the same as being wise; unless a country wants to be wise, it may not be rich and powerful long.

I do not think it can be said that education is irrelevant. The example of Prussia after the Napoleonic Wars and of Denmark after 1864 shows it is possible to achieve great social and political results through education. It also shows that it is possible for a country to make up its mind to have a kind of education that it never had before and to lift itself by its own bootstraps into a different spiritual world. This does not mean that the educational system can achieve these results behind the back of the population or against its wishes. It does mean that, if a country decides to move into a different spiritual world, it can use the educational system to help it get there. The educational system is a means to the achievement of the country's ideals. The decision about the ideals is made by the country, not by the educational system.

The Utopians decided that they wanted to be wise and established an educational system and a university to help them become so. They decided that what they needed was an educational system that trained them in the critical comprehension of important issues and a university that acted as a center of independent thought. The content of their curriculum, the organization of their educational institutions, and the freedom of their teachers are the necessary consequences of their fundamental decision. Though Utopia is a perfect country, no Utopian thinks it is: it is not wise to believe in your own perfection. The educational system and University of Utopia, therefore, far from being devoted to tribal self-adoration, are directed to throwing the clearest possible light upon the problems of mankind and of the conduct of Utopia with regard to them.

In the United States, that richest and most powerful of countries, is it possible to have the educational system and the University of Utopia? Not unless the people want them. Do they want them? It is hard to say. I think that in a kind of basic, unconscious way they do. In a kind of basic, unconscious way everybody everywhere would rather be wise than foolish. But think of the cost of the journey to Utopia. Think of the thought, the effort, and the drastic reorganization of our educational institutions. The most formidable task of all is that of persuading Americans to believe that they ought to want to become Utopians. The example of Prussia and Denmark suggest that thoroughgoing educational redirection may be possible only in a period of national humiliation. But progress by catastrophe is a repulsive doctrine: only a nihilist would favor catastrophe as a means of social reform.

Still I suggest that the imminence of catastrophe and the insoluble character of such problems as Korea and the atomic bomb might be sufficient to shock us out of our complacency, to set us to wondering whether riches and power are enough, and to start us on the journey to Utopia.

If we can start, what will sustain us on the way? I answer, "The spirit of our country." The deepest values of the American tradition are the deepest values of the West. They are the values of Utopia. Jefferson's resolution about the management of the University of Virginia must be regarded as the hasty act or momentary lapse of a politician bearing the scars of heavy fighting. Support for this view of his resolution is found in all his teachings from the Declaration of Independence onward. To Jefferson, America was to be Utopia. We can see now that he had not thought through the kind of university that Utopia required. But we can reach our own determination on that point in the light of the body of political doctrine that he left us.

The leading articles of the American faith are universal suffrage, universal education, independence of thought and action as the birthright of every individual, and reliance on reason as the principal means by which society is to be advanced. To the extent to which the American people have now forgotten or distorted these ideas, to that extent they have strayed from their own path. This was the path to Utopia.

When the history of our era is written, it may be that the last fifty years will be seen as a mere transitional period, during which a country rose suddenly to overwhelming wealth and power, built the framework of a vast educational system, committed many aberrations because of the size and complexity of its undertakings and the novelty of its problems, but always cherished the underlying convictions that were to come to flower in the next phase of its development. In that phase substance will be given to the forms, direction will be given to the machines, that have been designed in the transitional era of construction and expansion. That substance and direction can be drawn from the deepest values of America and the West.

In the long and painful journey to Utopia the American people have their own tradition, their own genius, their own spirit to guide them.